EDWARD II

For F. C. Troughton

EDWARD II
1307-1327

Mary Saaler

THE RUBICON PRESS

The Rubicon Press
57 Cornwall Gardens
London SW7 4BE

British Library Cataloguing-in-Publication Data

A catalogue record for this book is available from the British Library.

ISBN 0-948695-55-2 (hbk)
ISBN 0-948695-56-0 (pbk)

Printed and bound in Great Britain by Biddles Limited of Guildford
and King's Lynn

CONTENTS

CONTENTS (continued)

ILLUSTRATIONS

Cover: Detail from the alabaster tomb of Edward II in St Peter's Abbey, Gloucester, known as Gloucester Cathedral since the Reformation. (*D. Swan*).

Fourteen-century painting in Westminster Abbey, believed to be of Edward II. (*By courtesy of the Dean and Chapter of Westminster*).

The Coronation of a King, possibly Edward II. The King is shown sitting on his Coronation chair attended by priests and courtiers. The faces of the people can be seen looking through a grille on the top left. (*By courtesy of the Master and Fellows of Corpus Christi College, Cambridge*).

The Weeping King, believed to be Edward II, part of the tomb of John of Eltham in Westminster Abbey. *(By courtesy of the Dean and Chapter of Westminster)*.

Castle Rising, Norfolk, Queen Isabella's final residence. (*M. Saaler*).

Berkeley Castle, Gloucestershire, the scene of Edward II's murder. (*D. Swan*).

Edward II, King of England, and Isabella, daughter of Philip, King of France, depicted in a treatise by Walter de Milemete. (*By courtesy of The Governing Body of Christ Church, Oxford*).

The execution of Hugh Despenser the younger at Hereford. (*By courtesy of the Bibliothèque Nationale, Paris*).

Effigy of Edward II in Gloucester Cathedral. (*D. Swan*).

ACKNOWLEDGEMENTS

This book was written as a result of archaeological excavations at Bletchingley, in Surrey, and I should like to thank all the members of the Bourne Society Archaeological Group for their encouragement and support during the writing of *Edward II*. I am also grateful to the Surrey Archaeological Society for help in obtaining documents and to staff at the Gwent Record Office.

Thanks are also due to staff at University College London for their support and to Donald Swan for his photographic skills.

Furthermore, I wish to acknowledge permissions kindly granted to me by Gael and Toby Falk, William and Anne Browne, the Dean and Chapter of Westminster, the Master and Fellows of Corpus Christi College, Cambridge, the Governing Body of Christ Church, Oxford, the Manchester University Press and the Bibliothèque Nationale, Paris.

Finally, I am most grateful to staff and students of Latin Palaeography at the University of Keele and, in particular, to the Croxden Chronicle Group, whose patience and careful analysis have contributed greatly to this book.

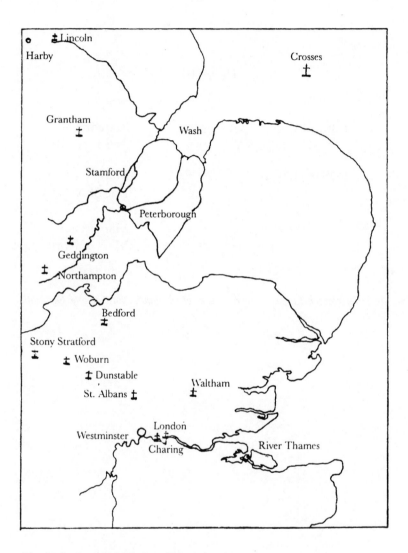

Map showing the route taken by Queen Eleanor's funeral procession.

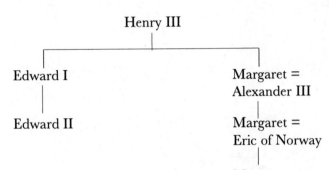

Family connections between the royal houses of England, Norway and Scotland.

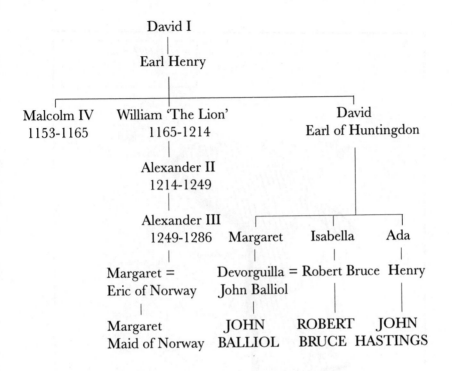

Family connections of the three main claimants to the Scottish throne.

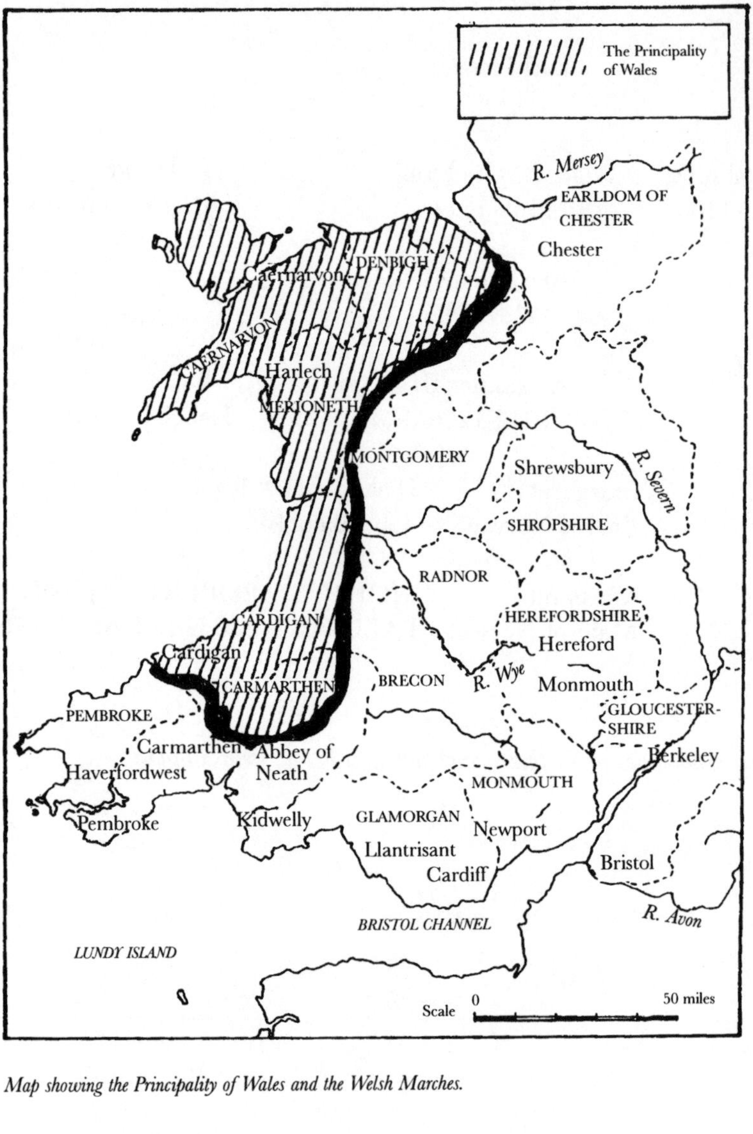
The Principality of Wales
R. Mersey
EARLDOM OF CHESTER
Chester
DENBIGH
Caernarvon
CAERNARVON
Harlech
MERIONETH
MONTGOMERY
Shrewsbury
R. Severn
SHROPSHIRE
RADNOR
HEREFORDSHIRE
Hereford
CARDIGAN
Cardigan
CARMARTHEN
BRECON
R. Wye
Monmouth
GLOUCESTER-SHIRE
Berkeley
PEMBROKE
Carmarthen
Abbey of Neath
Haverfordwest
MONMOUTH
Pembroke
Kidwelly
GLAMORGAN
Newport
Llantrisant
Cardiff
Bristol
R. Avon
BRISTOL CHANNEL
LUNDY ISLAND
Scale
0
50 miles

Map showing the Principality of Wales and the Welsh Marches.

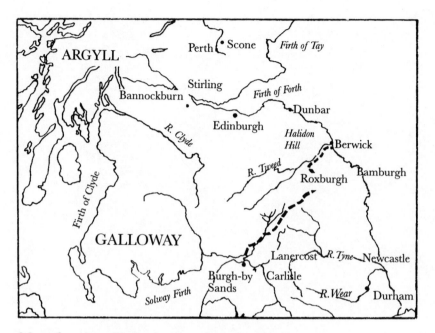

Map of northern England and southern Scotland.

INTRODUCTION

In 1307, the reign of Edward II opened with high hopes. Contemporaries looked with favour at this excellent Prince of Wales; he was tall, strong and handsome; the kingdom was prosperous. The omens were good. But his unconventional behaviour soon dashed these expectations. He was not interested in horsemanship or fighting; he took delight in the countryside; he enjoyed 'rustic' pursuits, like thatching, hedging and ditching. He loved music and his pastimes included woodwork and metalwork. Above all, his affection for Piers Gavaston and Hugh Despenser the younger threatened both him and his kingdom.[1] Over the years he has been viewed as: 'a big, dull, unmannerly oaf'; 'destitute of all those qualities which constitute Edward I's claim to greatness'; 'a scatter-brained wastrel'; 'totally unfit to rule'; 'a brutal and brainless athlete'; 'lazy and incapable'.[2]

The chronicle of Ranulf Higden, known as the 'monk of Chester', was particularly brutal. It described Edward as handsome and physically strong but weak in character. He was not interested in the companionship of noblemen but sought out the company of harlots, singers and actors, drivers, labourers, rowers, sailors and other craftsmen. He drank a great deal, betrayed secrets, struck out at bystanders for no particular reason and followed the advice of others, rather than using his own judgement. The writer went on to depict him as excessively generous, lavish in entertainments, quick to speak, unstable, unsuccessful against his enemies and cruel to his servants. He was deeply attached to one of his friends, a man whom he adored, enriched, honoured and made great. This passion brought disaster to the lover and disgrace to the object of his love. It caused offence to the people and damage to the kingdom.[3] This view of Edward was probably first written down in the 1320s, soon after the events it describes. As a measure of the writer's reliability, he was called to court by Edward III in 1352 and asked to provide historical evidence, which suggests that 'his reputation as an historian was well established'.[4]

Ralph Holinshed's chronicle, first published in the 1570s, followed the same trend. It implied that, as a young man, Edward's interests were somewhat trivial 'he was of nature given to lightness' but, with proper guidance, this 'lightness' might be turned to good effect. It also suggested that Edward was playing a role, sometimes pretending to be serious, virtuous and modest but, under the influence of Gavaston, he ignored 'the good government of the commonwealth and gave himself to wantonness, passing his time in voluptuous pleasure and riotous excess'. Gavaston was depicted as the evil influence,

> who furnished his court with companies of jesters, ruffians, flattering parasites, musicians and other naughty ribalds, that the King might spend both days and nights in jesting, playing, blanketing and other such filthy and dishonourable exercises.[5]

Christopher Marlowe, in his play *Edward II*, which was produced about 1590, followed Holinshed's view. He presented a weak and doomed King, overshadowed by stronger men. Most of these comments were coloured by hindsight, justified by Edward's tragic death. To his contemporaries, he looked like a King and they admired his handsome appearance. But they were truly puzzled by his unusual, unkinglike personality and his overwhelming affection for his favourites.[6] Professor Tout's study of Edward II, first published in 1914, suggested that contemporaries complained more about the King's idleness and incompetence than about his vices:

> If he did not like work, he was not very vicious; he stuck loyally to his friends and was fairly harmless, being nobody's enemy so much as his own.[7]

In 1980, Michael Prestwich considered that 'Edward II was one of the most unsuccessful Kings ever to rule England', but went on to say, 'Yet the reign has its fascination. The failures of a society often reveal its essential character better than the successes'.[8]

Pierre Chaplais, writing in 1994, expressed much the same view as Tout, suggesting that Edward was 'not so much an incompetent King, as a reluctant one'.[9] Twentieth-century fiction offers the traditional picture of a worthless King:

> Edward II was as unfit to rule as his father had been outstanding. He infuriated the magnates by ignoring them in favour of his favourites. He was thought to be a homosexual.[10]

Maurice Druon described his unspeakable behaviour through the eyes of Queen Isabella:

Edward brings the lowest and most infamous men to the Palace. He visits the low dens of the Port of London, sits with tramps, wrestles with lightermen, races against grooms. Fine tournaments, these, for our delectation! He has no care who runs the kingdom, provided his pleasures are organized and shared.[11]

Contemporaries found it difficult to understand how the King was not content with occupations suited to his status, such as hunting, battles, politics or business, in the company of his noblemen. Instead, he deliberately avoided them and sought out men who would participate with him in the 'lowly' pastimes of racing, rowing, acting, thatching and digging.[12]

The sources for the reign of Edward II can be divided into two main groups. The first group is formed from the records of the official departments of the royal administration, consisting of the Exchequer (the office of finance) and the Chancery (the secretarial office under the control of the Chancellor, who was, in effect, the King's chief minister). However, there was a great deal of overlap between the official departments and the private administration of the Household, consisting of the Chamber, headed by the Chamberlain, which was concerned with finance, and the Wardrobe, which dealt with domestic administration. Nominally, these were separate departments but, in practice, their roles frequently overlapped. While many of the records contain financial information, they also contain large amounts of general correspondence. Legal documents, the records of Parliament and the registers of Archbishops and Bishops provide additional information.[13]

The second group of records consists chiefly of chronicles. A chronicle has been described as a mixture of a history book and a newspaper, offering a sense of the past linked with the present. Many religious establishments compiled their own chronicles of past events and added to them in the course of time. Since these were recorded in more or less chronological order, they provided a useful work of reference for future generations. In addition, copies of chronicles were circulated among monasteries, where writers took extracts from earlier versions and added their own information.

Some works, such as Higden's *Polychronicon*, the anonymous *Life of Edward the Second* and the chronicle compiled by Adam Murimuth, who was in royal service, were written first-hand, soon after the events they described. Various later writers then incorporated these chronicles into their own historical studies. The Abbey of St Albans was a particularly influential centre for the compilation of historical information. During the thirteenth century the Abbey produced the *Flores Historiarum*, which was

3

continued at Westminster Abbey in the early fourteenth century, providing contemporary evidence for the reign of Edward II. The tradition of writing chronicles was revived at St Albans towards the end of the fourteenth century when Thomas Walsingham compiled his *Historia Anglicana*, using many of these earlier sources. Chronicles produced in the north of England, for instance, the *Anonimalle Chronicle*, which was produced at St Mary's Abbey, York, and the *Chronicle of Lanercost*, written in Cumberland, provide a valuable balance to those produced in and around London. While chronicles may be unreliable about dates and details, they give colour and background to the personalities and events of the period. Fourteenth-century poems and political songs also provide valuable contemporary views.[14]

I EDWARD OF CAERNARVON

On St Mark's day, April 25th, 1284, Edward, the son of King Edward I, was born in north Wales, at Caernarvon. He was the fourth son of Edward I and Eleanor of Castile, but the omens for his future survival were not good; two elder brothers, John and Henry, had already died, while Alphonso, the heir to the throne, died later that same year at the age of 12, leaving Edward as the only male heir. The young Edward grew up with five surviving sisters, Eleanor, Joan, Margaret, Mary, and Elizabeth, who was his junior by just two years. These children, and the others who did not survive beyond childhood, were so beautiful that their grandfather, Henry III, gave Eleanor of Castile an extra allowance from his Privy Purse for producing such a handsome brood of children.[1]

Following his birth at Caernarvon, the young Edward was known as Edward of Caernarvon, or the Lord Edward. He was born against a background of warfare. Caernarvon was the ancient centre for north Wales, captured by Edward I in May 1283. The castle that he built became a symbol of his conquest of the whole country. To organize his conquered lands, he issued *The Statute of Wales* which remained the basis of administration in Wales for centuries afterwards. Under the new system, many old laws were kept, but some were abolished, others were changed and new ones were added to comply with English laws and customs. Wales was divided into counties and county courts were set up, establishing the same administrative system as in England.

Caernarvon itself was full of symbolism, being the supposed burial place of Constantius, father of the Roman Emperor, Constantine. Traces of the Roman fort of Segontium could still be seen, providing evidence for the strategic importance of the site and a visible reminder of an imperial power and earlier conquest.[2] By the time of Edward's birth, the King's new town of Caernarvon was beginning to take shape and the castle was under construction. The first buildings were timber-framed lodgings for the King and Queen and, by August 1283, stonemasons were being summoned to work on the castle. Enough of the structure was ready and fit for the King and Queen to spend the great festival of Easter there in April 1284. After Easter, the King returned to Rhuddlan Castle leaving the Queen at Caernarvon, where Edward was born about two weeks later. A major part of the castle was completed by 1292 but the Welsh forces rose in rebellion and sacked it in 1294, as a protest against this powerful symbol of conquest. It was left empty and derelict for about six months, but it was then rebuilt and remained the administrative centre for north Wales until the seventeenth century.[3]

The attractive legend of Edward I presenting the Welsh people with a Prince who was born in Wales and could speak no English did not become widespread until the sixteenth century. The story was first published in 1580, in John Stow's *Chronicle of England*. Certainly, there is no factual evidence for the event but perhaps Stow was repeating some earlier tradition that then became accepted as fact. The legend probably arose because people formed a link between the place of Edward's birth and the formal charter which gave him the title and the Principality of Wales at the age of 16. Although the charter may have been an official recognition of an earlier grant, it would be unusual to make this gift to Edward at the time of his birth, when his elder brother Alphonso, who was the heir to the throne, had not received a similar award.[4]

The new baby was baptized on May 1st 1284. He was named Edward after his father; the name also linked him with Edward the Confessor, the English royal saint. Later that same year, as a further example of the symbolism of conquest, Alphonso placed on the tomb of Edward the Confessor at Westminster Abbey a gold crown and other precious items that had been taken from Llewellyn ap Gruffydd, one of the defeated Welsh princes.[5]

Edward's first nurse may have been a Welshwoman. Many years later Mary Maunsel of Caernarvon, who was described as 'the King's nurse', received a grant of money to allow her to return to Wales. In 1312 she was receiving £5 a year from the profits of royal mills at Caernarvon and was holding property there in 1317, rent-free.[6] However, she was his nurse for only a few months and, perhaps because of ill-health, she was replaced by an English woman, Alice Leygrave. Alice remained in royal service and both she and her daughter, Cecilia, were later in the court of Edward's wife, Queen Isabella. Alice and her relations were well-rewarded for their loyalty with generous grants of property from the royal family.[7]

Edward was brought up with his five sisters. After the death of Alphonso, he was the only boy in the family until after his father remarried in 1299. When the King was abroad, John of Brabant, son of the Duke of Brabant, stayed in England and lived with the royal children as a substitute elder brother. John was betrothed to Margaret, one of Edward's sisters, and later married her. Giles of Audenarde, later replaced by Adam of Blyth, was responsible for keeping the accounts of the royal children's Wardrobe and Household. These men recorded the day-to-day expenses of the 'Lord

Edward and the King's daughters'. There were payments to the clerks who kept the records, and to others, including the butler, carter, cook, laundress and tailors. There were frequent references to cloth being bought for the children's clothes, such as cloth of gold, silks, furs and wool. The bills for food included payments for sugar loaves, sugar candy, fresh fruit, spices, nuts and baskets of dried fruit, and figs and raisins imported from Spain.[8]

As well as the companionship of officials of the Household, Edward had young male friends of roughly the same age. For example, there was William Comyn, a member of the powerful Scottish family of the Earls of Buchan, and the accounts show that he, too, received an allowance for his clothes, his saddles, bridles, sheets and linen for the year 1290.[9] As Edward's sisters grew up, they gradually left the royal family to form marriage alliances elsewhere. His eldest sister, Eleanor, who was twenty years older than Edward, first followed up her mother's marriage connections with Spain and was betrothed to Alphonso, the heir to the Kingdom of Aragon, but when he died, she contracted a French alliance and left England in 1293 to marry Henry, Count of Bar. The next sister, Joan, was called Joan of Acre, because she had been born at Acre, in Syria, while Edward I and Queen Eleanor were on a crusade to the Holy Land. At first Joan was betrothed to Hartman, the heir to the Hapsburg throne, but he died in 1281 and in 1290 she married Gilbert of Clare, Earl of Gloucester. The Pope granted a dispensation for the marriage, since the Earl had been previously married to a cousin of the King. Margaret, the third sister, married John of Brabant in the same year. The two weddings were celebrated in London in magnificent style. Margaret remained in England until 1297 when she left to join her husband in the Netherlands.

Edward's sister, Mary, entered a convent when she was seven years old. Her grandmother, Eleanor of Provence, was already patron of the Priory at Amesbury in Wiltshire, and Eleanor became a nun there six months after Mary entered the convent. As a baby, Edward travelled with the rest of the royal family on visits to Canterbury, Lewes and Chichester, finally reaching Amesbury, where he was present at his sister's consecration in August 1285. But living in a convent did not prevent Mary from taking part in court festivities and she often joined her sisters at court. According to Green's *Lives of the Princesses of England*, Mary spent her life devoted to pleasure. 'In the furniture of her apartments, in the luxuries of her table and the extent of her stud, Mary rivalled the splendour of the court of Edward I'. She loved music and enjoyed gambling. However, her presence at the convent helped to preserve a close connection between the Priory and the royal family and she used her influence to benefit the nuns. Edward's youngest sister, Elizabeth, married John, Count of Holland and

Zeeland. He died two years later and she then married Humphrey Bohun, Earl of Hereford.[10]

Edward's tutor, from about the age of 11 until his nineteenth birthday, was Guy Ferrer. Ferrer had already been in the service of the Queen and, as a man with experience of both military and court life, he was appointed *magister* (tutor) to the King's son. In 1295 he was recorded as 'staying continually in the company of Edward, the King's son, by special order'.[11] Langley, in Hertfordshire, was the settled winter home of these royal children, while they often spent the summer months travelling, mostly through southern England. For example, in 1289, Edward stayed at places near London; he was at Fulham and at Kennington, he also went to the Tower of London, where he probably saw the royal menagerie, which included a lion, a leopard and a bear. Such animals were gifts to the royal family from foreign monarchs. In addition, Edward went to Northfleet in Kent and he and his sisters went to Dover to greet their parents on their return from Gascony.[12] The country house at Winsdor was also a favourite residence for the royal family. It lay in an extensive park about five miles from the castle and traces of the moat can still be seen. Edward spent much time there in his early years and continued to enjoy staying there after he became King.[13] But from November to March the royal children generally stayed at Langley. Queen Eleanor held the manor of Langley from Edmund, Earl of Cornwall, cousin of Edward I. During the reign of Edward I, it was known simply as Langley; the first reference to it as 'King's Langley' did not appear until 1428. It lies just over 20 miles to the north-west of London and about seven miles from both the magnificent Benedictine Abbey at St Albans and Berkhamsted Castle, which was also a royal house.

Between 1271 and 1289 extensive work was done at Langley to make it comfortable for the royal family. Stone was brought in from quarries at Reigate in Surrey and the accounts referred to payments for timber, tiles and iron. Work was carried out on apartments for the King and Queen and for their eldest son, Alphonso. A new garden was also laid out there. A valuation of the manor in 1291 describes the main house, set in gardens and meadows, with a park, fishponds and water mills. During the 1290s, changes were made in the great hall when two new chimneys were added and the walls were whitewashed and then painted in bright colours of red and yellow. Alexander, the royal painter, worked there for 52 days at the rate of 4d a day and another painter came during the summer, while the royal family was away, to decorate the walls of the great hall with paintings of 54 shields and a scene of knights riding to a tournament. At the same time, some of the private rooms were made more comfortable by the addition of extra fireplaces. The surrounding gardens contained fruit trees and the estate also had two parks, which either held deer or were used as pasture for other animals. There were extensive stables which contained a camel, in addition to the horses. The young Edward had his own apartments at Langley and there is evidence of his interest in music, since the organist of the Earl of Surrey came to Langley to repair an organ for him in 1303.[14]

However, the royal presence at Langley was not always welcome to the local people. The chronicler of St Peter's Priory at Dunstable, about 12 miles distant, complained about the effect of the young Edward's Household on local trade in 1294. He described how the market at Dunstable and other markets and the surrounding countryside were severely affected by the long period of residence of Edward at Langley and St Albans:

> Two hundred dishes a day were not enough for his kitchen. Whatever he spent on himself or his followers, he took without paying for it. His officials took all the supplies that came to the market, even cheese and eggs, and not only whatever was for sale, but they even took things not for sale that were in the houses of the townspeople. They scarcely left anybody a tally (receipt). They took bread from the bakers and beer from the ale-wives or, if they had none, they forced them to make bread and beer.[15]

In spite of any local ill-feeling, Langley was a favourite house with the royal family. The chronicler, William Risinger, recorded that in 1299,

> As All Saints' Day approached, the King and Queen, having summoned the Bishop of Norwich, the Abbot of St. Albans, the Count of Savoy and many others, celebrated the feast of All Saints at Langley.[16]

This was the place where young Edward spent most of his youth and, after the Earl of Cornwall died without leaving any heirs, the King granted the manor to his son in 1302.[17] It remained the favourite private home of Edward of Caernarvon until his death in 1327. It was last occupied in about 1476 and subsequently fell into decay; only a few fragments of masonry now remain.

As his sisters married and moved away, young Edward also lost his mother and grandmother in quick succession. His mother, Eleanor of Castile, was often absent while she accompanied her husband on his travels in this country and abroad. After the Queen had travelled with the King on a journey that took them through Cheshire and Derbyshire, she fell ill and died at Harby in Nottinghamshire on November 28th 1290. Her death had a devastating effect on her husband. He missed her deeply and to commemorate her life, he commanded that her body be taken first to Lincoln, where her entrails and heart were removed for separate burials. The entrails were buried in Lincoln Cathedral, where a tomb was later set up in 1293. At her own request, her heart was buried at Blackfriars in London within the Dominican priory where the heart of her young son, Alphonso, had been placed six years earlier. The remains of her body and her heart were brought from Lincoln to Westminster Abbey in twelve stages.

The King and his courtiers accompanied the body on this sad journey for most of the way. At each place where the funeral procession stopped for the night, the King ordered a stone cross to be set up in memory of the Queen. The mourners halted in Lincolnshire, at Lincoln, Grantham and Stamford. When they reached Northamptonshire, they stopped at Geddington and Northampton. In Buckinghamshire they halted at Stony Stratford; in Bedfordshire they stopped at Woburn and Dunstable. The chronicler of Dunstable recorded the passage of the funeral procession: it remained at the Priory for one night and the monks provided silk brocades to form a canopy over her body. The mourners then reached St Albans, not far from Langley, and from there they travelled to Waltham, in Essex. Waltham Cross was built at the place where the procession turned from the main road to the north to stay for the night at the Abbey of The Holy Cross. Finally, the mourners reached London, halting at Cheapside and then at the royal mews at Charing.[18] In addition to the crosses, the King wished to set up tombs for his wife at Lincoln, Blackfriars and Westminster. The two main monuments were at Lincoln and Westminster. The tomb at Lincoln was destroyed during the Commonwealth, but a drawing shows that it was probably the same as the Westminster memorial. There seems to be no surviving drawing or description of the monument at Blackfriars. Colvin comments on the effigy at Westminster, made of Purbeck marble and gilt bronze, 'the superb workmanship (makes) it one of the most perfect of all monuments to medieval royalty'.

Of the twelve crosses, only three have survived in their original form –at Geddington, Northampton and Waltham. The two London crosses were probably the most elaborate since they were the most costly, being made largely of expensive Purbeck marble.[19] The King mourned deeply for a remarkable woman. During the 36 years of their marriage they were rarely separated; she accompanied her husband on a crusade in 1270 and gave birth to a daughter on the journey. Edward of Caernarvon was born while the Queen was in Wales, travelling on campaign with the King.

When Edward was just five years old, he travelled with his sisters from Langley to Dover to meet his parents on their return from one of their journeys to the continent. It had lasted for three years.

The young Edward lost his mother in 1290 when he was six years old; the following year, his grandmother, Eleanor of Provence, also died. While the children's mother travelled with the King, their grandmother had kept a kindly eye on their welfare. Her protective attitude was not surprising when so many of her grandchildren had died in infancy. She had written to the King in protest when she discovered that he was intending to take his only son with him on one of his northern journeys and she suggested that the child would benefit from staying in the south during the autumn months. Although Eleanor had retired to the convent at Amesbury, she did not fail to watch over her grandchildren until her death in 1291. As the various members of young Edward's family either died or moved away, he gradually emerged from a fairly secluded private life to become a public figure, as the heir to the throne.[20]

II MARRIAGE PLANS

Edward's marriage was of crucial importance. In the ten years between 1289 and 1299, the King proposed three marriage alliances for his son, first with Scotland and, when that failed, with Flanders and, finally, with France. In 1289 Edward I obtained, in his son's name, a dispensation from Pope Nicholas IV that would allow Edward of Caernarvon to marry Margaret, the daughter of the King of Norway, who was also the heiress to the throne of Scotland.[1] Alexander III, King of Scotland, had married Margaret, the sister of Edward I, they had two sons who both died before inheriting the throne. There was a strong element of personal friendship between Alexander and Edward and the English King had sent letters to Alexander to express his sorrow at the death of his heir, who was also Edward's nephew.[2] Their deaths left just a daughter, another Margaret, who had married Eric, King of Norway, in 1281. But this Queen Margaret died in 1283, leaving a baby daughter, also called Margaret, who became known as 'The Maid of Norway' or 'The Damsel of Scotland'. When Alexander III died in 1286, this young girl was heiress to the thrones of both Scotland and Norway. In effect, a marriage between Edward of Caernarvon and Margaret of Norway might have united the three kingdoms of England, Scotland and Norway. Since the prospective bride and groom were related to the third degree of kinship, a dispensation from the Pope was necessary before such an alliance could be made.

After the dispensation was granted, the King appointed Anthony Bek, Bishop of Durham, John, Earl of Surrey, and Henry Newark, Dean of York, to act as his proctors in negotiating with the King of Norway. In April 1290 letters were sent to Eric urging him to send his daughter without delay. Later that year, an agreement was made to pay to Norway the sum of £400 every year until Margaret reached the age of 15. During the absence and minority of the young Queen, six Scottish noblemen, known as the Guardians, formed a regency council to take control. In June 1290, the King wrote to the Guardians of Scotland and the 'whole community of Scotland', promising to maintain the laws and customs of the country after the marriage. He said that the seal of King Alexander should be used until Margaret arrived when a new seal would be made and kept by the

Chancellor of Scotland. If there was no marriage, Edward promised to send back Margaret to be Queen of Scotland.[3]

The practical arrangements were set in hand. A 'great ship' was made ready at Great Yarmouth. The supplies included wine, beer, meat, dried fish, peas, and beans, together with nuts, dried fruits, sugar and spices. This was followed by a second expedition, carrying more casks of wine to Norway. Margaret set out on her journey from Bergen to Scotland, but she did not long survive the voyage. Some versions of the story claim that she died at sea; others say that she died after the ship landed at Kirkwall in Orkney. This is probably the true version, since the Bishop of St Andrew's reported the arrival of the 'Damsel of Scotland' in Orkney during August 1290. The first news of her death reached London on October 7th when messengers arrived from the Bishop. Ironically, the papal bull for the marriage was presented for enrolment at Westminster just two days later, on October 9th.[4] In the event, her body was placed in St Magnus' Cathedral in Kirkwall before being taken back to Bergen for burial. She was seven years old at the time.[5] The death of Margaret ended the possibility of a close alliance between England and Scotland.[6] If this marriage had taken place, the final union between England and Scotland would probably have occurred much sooner than it did. There were strong ties between the two countries and the marriage treaty allowed Scotland to retain its own laws and customs, unlike Wales. The death of Margaret brought great upheaval in Scotland, with no less than 13 people stating their claim to the vacant throne. Only three of these had a genuine claim, tracing their descent from David, Earl of Huntingdon, who was the brother of William the Lion, King of Scotland. Huntingdon had three daughters and from these came the three rival claimants. John Balliol was a descendant of the eldest daughter; the grandson of the second one was Robert Bruce, and the descendant of the third was John Hastings. Problems associated with the Scottish throne were to occupy both Edward I and Edward II for many years to come.

After the marriage alliance with Scotland failed, Edward I turned his attention to Flanders to find a bride for his son. His marriage plans formed part of an attack on France after Philip IV, King of France, had annexed the Duchy of Gascony in 1294. Gascony lay in south-west France and, as part of Aquitaine, it had belonged to the Kings of England since Henry II married Eleanor of Aquitaine in 1152. However, Guy of Dampierre, Count of Flanders, was a vassal of Philip IV but was eager to oppose his overlord's territorial ambitions. Edward I saw an advantage in promoting this dispute and, in June 1294, there were plans for a marriage between Philippa, daughter of Dampierre, and Edward of Caernarvon. Because of strong opposition from the French King, it took three years to finalize the arrangements. Eventually, on February 2nd 1297, at Walsingham in Norfolk, Dampierre's three proctors swore on his behalf to uphold the alliance. A few days later, three English proctors swore to a betrothal between Edward and Phillipa, or her sister Isabella as a substitute. However, Edward I abandoned the Flemish marriage when he discovered that an alliance with Flanders might be a liability. By 1297 it was becoming obvious that support for Dampierre would involve England in financial and military commitments that were not acceptable. And so, in 1298 at Edward's request, Pope Boniface VIII annulled the marriage contract. But to confirm the truce lately made with France, a double marriage alliance was made. In 1299 Edward I married Margaret, sister of Philip IV, while a betrothal was made between Edward of Caernarvon, then aged 15, and Isabella, Philip's daughter. This final alliance was cemented by marriage but it brought great unhappiness to both parties.[7]

III EDWARD OF CAERNARVON AND SCOTLAND

Edward I left his son a legacy of unfinished business concerning Scotland. Following the death of the Maid of Norway, three men, John Balliol, Robert Bruce and John Hastings, were the main claimants to the Scottish throne. Hastings further complicated matters by asserting that Scotland should be divided between these three men. The Guardians of Scotland referred the decision to Edward I and, on May 10th 1291, an assembly was held at Norham in Northumberland under the King's presidency. At the assembly a commission was set up to give judgement. The commissioners decided that John Balliol, being the son of the eldest daughter of the Earl of Huntingdon, was the rightful King of Scotland. Balliol then accepted the throne and did homage to Edward I, acknowledging him as overlord. However, the Scottish noblemen were dissatisfied when they discovered that Edward's ideas of feudal rights threatened the independence that he had promised them. They incited Balliol to assert the independence of Scotland and war seemed inevitable. A secret treaty was drawn up between Scotland and France, who were united in their opposition to England. In reply to this threat, Edward I embarked on a campaign of conquest to reduce the Scots to submission. He fought against the Scottish army at Dunbar in East Lothian and captured Dunbar Castle. Balliol was forced to concede defeat and he surrendered his crown. At the end of 1296, Edward I left the Earl of Surrey in Scotland as regent and returned to London. The Scottish coronation stone was removed from Scone Abbey in Tayside, the traditional site of enthronement for the Kings of Scotland. As a symbol of conquest, it was placed beneath the English coronation chair in Westminster Abbey in London, where it remained for 700 years. The war was ostensibly over.

However, the Scots were not willing to accept Balliol's surrender. William Wallace raised a Scottish force, supported by Robert Bruce, the grandson of Robert Bruce, the former claimant to the throne. In the spring of 1297 they launched a combined attack against English rule while Edward I was in Gascony. Wallace and his supporters destroyed the English army under the Earl of Surrey and ravaged the countryside of Northumberland as far south as Newcastle. Balliol was still held captive in the Tower of London, but the rebels claimed to be acting in his name. Edward I hurriedly returned from Gascony and was in Scotland by June 1298. The two sides met at Falkirk, in the Forth valley, where the Scottish force was defeated in a hard-fought battle. But Edward I did not have sufficient forces to follow up his success; as he moved to the south, the Scots recaptured Stirling. Robert Bruce, John Comyn and the Bishop of St Andrew's now took on the roles of Guardians of Scotland. Comyn had married into the Balliol family and so was regarded as John Balliol's representative in Scotland. The Guardians appealed for help to the Pope on the grounds that Scotland lay within the jurisdiction of the papal court. In 1300 the Pope sent a letter to Edward I demanding that disputes between the two countries should be referred to Rome for settlement. Edward reacted by angrily rejecting papal intervention.

During the King's absence on campaign, young Edward had taken charge of military forces in England, at least in name, if not in reality. In March 1296, when Edward I was campaigning in Scotland, there was fear of a French attack on southern England. Faced with this threat, the citizens of London raised a force to guard the coastline near Dover. This force was placed under the command of Edward of Caernarvon, who was then 11 years old. The invasion did not take place, but Lord Edward was considered to be in nominal control of an armed force. The following year, when the King spent seven months in Flanders, he again left his son nominally in charge. In reality, the country was ruled by a regency council, but Edward of Caernarvon witnessed documents and put his seal to them.[1]

During the King's absence, Wallace's victories had boosted the hopes of the Scots and a Scottish war was again threatening. Edward of Caernarvon was faced with having to lead an army against the Scots at the age of 12. Writs were sent out in October summoning a large force to Newcastle to go with Edward of Caernarvon against the Scots. But, by this time, Edward I had abandoned his ideas of supporting a Flemish revolt against the King of France and he made a truce with Philip. Edward I wrote saying that he would return to England to lead the Scottish campaigns in person. As a result, Edward of Caernarvon was left to while away his time at Langley, instead of leading an army into Scotland.

It was only in 1300 that Edward I decided that his son should accompany him on a Scottish campaign. Edward of Caernarvon was then 16 years old. The forces were summoned to meet at Carlisle to be ready at midsummer. Queen Margaret, like her predecessor, Queen Eleanor, accompanied the King on his campaigns, and the various members of royal party set out from St Albans after Easter. They made a leisurely journey northwards, visiting St Edmund's Abbey at Bury St Edmunds, in

Suffolk. Young Edward stayed there a week longer than his father. He seems to have enjoyed his visit and the chronicler recorded:

> The King's son stayed longer, enjoying the seclusion of the monastery. He became our brother in chapter. The magnificence of the place and the frequent recreation of the brethren pleased him greatly. Every day, he asked to be served with a monk's portion, such as the brothers take in the refectory. Some say that he declared that he had never enjoyed the pleasant company of monks so much. But on the twelfth day, he said farewell to the monks and hurried to join his father.[2]

As the royal party advanced towards Scotland, the Queen stayed at Brotherton, near Pontefract, in Yorkshire, where she gave birth to a son on June 1st 1300. Edward of Caernarvon waited at Monk Frystone, just a few miles away, while the King rushed to see the new-born baby 'like a falcon before the wind'. The baby was named Thomas of Brotherton.[3] Edward seems to have been delighted to hear that he now had a half-brother, since he rewarded the messenger with a gift of £20 and sent a smaller sum to the new baby's nurses.[4] By the middle of June, the royal party reached Durham, where Lord Edward made an offering at the shrine of St Cuthbert in Durham Cathedral. On June 25th they arrived at Carlisle. Reinforcements came to join them from all directions. Supplies also poured into the north-west by sea, especially from the Irish ports. The *Song of Caerlaverock* emphasized the splendour of the assembled force. This song was composed by a herald who was serving in the King's army. It gives names and descriptions of all the nobles and knights who were present, providing a colourful, if extravagant, picture of the occasion. The composer described the knights riding on horses decked with brightly embroidered trappings and carrying their banners high on their lances. Their tents, too, were of bright colours and strewn with fresh flowers:

> And the King and his great household
> Immediately set forth against the Scots,
> Not in coats and surcoats,
> But on powerful and costly chargers,
> In order that they might not be taken by surprise,
> Well and securely armed.
> Mountains and valleys were everywhere
> Covered with sumpter horses and waggons
> With provisions and the train

Of the tents and pavilions,
And the days were long and fine.

Edward of Caernarvon was included in the list:

A youth of seventeen years of age
And newly bearing arms,
He was of a well proportioned and handsome person
Of a courteous disposition.[5]

They set out northwards from Carlisle on July 4th and the army increased in size as it went on its way. The King was intending to move westwards to invade Galloway, an area which supported both Bruce and Balliol. Before a full-scale attack was launched, the King decided to capture Caerlaverock Castle to safeguard the rear. The castle was situated on the northern shore of the Solway Firth, nine miles south of Dumfries, lying on low ground, protected by marshes and the sea. Because of its position, the King was able to use ships to bring his siege-engines close to the castle. It was typical of him to make extensive use of ships to support his army, hiring a large number of them and their masters from the Cinque Ports and other maritime towns.[6]

The attacking force was divided into four; Henry Lacy, Earl of Lincoln, led the vanguard; the Earl of Surrey led the next group; the King took the third group and Edward of Caernarvon commanded the rearguard. This was his first experience of command in battle, but trusted and experienced soldiers were all around him, especially John St John, who knew the area well. The attack lasted for a few days and the castle was captured, not by individual acts of bravery, but by being battered into surrender by siege-engines. One of these fearsome machines was distinguished by the name of Robinet. A chronicler recorded how the battering-rams and siege-engines crushed the defenders, destroyed the joints of the walls and undermined them, causing the castle to fall. With the rear now secure, the troops advanced into Galloway. However, in circumstances where the weather was poor and food was short, many soldiers deserted. There were a few skirmishes and ambushes, but the Scots were able to melt away into a familiar landscape and so avoid defeat. By August 15th the King had advanced as far as Wigtown, which lies about 40 miles west of Caerlaverock. From there, he turned back and left Scotland. In reality, the campaign had achieved very little.[7]

While staying in the north, the King summoned the Queen to join him and they stayed at Rose Castle and Holme Cultram Abbey in Cumberland. Edward of Caernarvon accompanied the royal party but, from time to time, left them to visit other nearby places, such as Penrith. During his time there, he had the chance to listen to music played on a harp and he was entertained by Martinettus, a Gascon jester. He passed time gambling with dice and he was pleased to receive the gift of two greyhounds, sent to him from north Wales by the constable of Conwy Castle. It was always characteristic of Edward to be kind and generous to people he liked and on one occasion he organized treatment for one of his carpenters, who was injured while working for him during the campaign.[8]

On November 1st, the English and Scots drew up a truce to last until Whitsun the following year. By November 3rd the English had returned to Carlisle and then moved southwards. The royal party stayed at Northampton for Christmas and, a fortnight later, Edward of Caernarvon was back at Langley. He travelled to the Augustinian College at Ashridge in Buckinghamshire where he took the King's place at the burial of the heart and flesh of Edmund, Earl of Cornwall, the King's cousin, who had died the previous September. This was a specially important ceremony, since the Earl of Cornwall had been the founder of the college. The Earl had no children and, on his death, his property reverted to the Crown. Langley was part of his estates, which Edward then acquired.[9]

IV   PRINCE OF WALES

Although the King was preoccupied with national affairs, he gave time to consider the status of his son and heir and perhaps he felt that Edward, at the age of 16, deserved a reward for his part in the Scottish campaigns. A charter, dated February 7th 1301, granted Edward the overlordship of royal lands in Wales and the earldom of Chester. Such a grant may be seen as a reward for past services and an acknowledgement of his future responsibilities.[1]

The Welsh lands were in two groups: the first group stretched across north Wales and included Gwynedd and Anglesey, while the second allocation lay in west and south Wales. With these came the castles and manors of Haverford and Builth and all other lands which were then in the King's hands, except the town and castle of Montgomery, which remained the property of Queen Margaret. However, by May 1301, this had changed and Edward also received Montgomery, while the Queen was granted other lands in exchange. In addition to the Welsh lands, Edward acquired the earldom of Chester. There had been Earls of Chester since the time of the Norman conquest but the lands had been part of the royal domains for about the last 70 years. The castles of Caernarvon, Carmarthen and Chester were the administrative centres for Edward's holdings. These huge grants of lands echoed those which the King himself had received from his own father, Henry III.

Once the Principality of Wales was held by the King's son, he might legitimately be called Prince of Wales, since he had taken over the lands of the former Welsh princes. The charter, which was issued in February, with the first grant of lands, did not mention the words 'Principality' or 'Prince'; it was not until the grant of Montgomery in May 1301 that the title 'Prince of Wales' was first applied to Edward. On April 6th 1301 Edward left Worcestershire and set out to 'inspect the land of Wales given to him by the King'.[2] He remained in the west for nearly five weeks, accepting homage and fealty from his tenants. To begin with, he stayed at Chester Castle, where he ordered some alterations to be made to make it more comfortable. He also commissioned a painter, William of Northampton, to paint a picture for the small chapel near the great hall, depicting the popular theme of the murder of Thomas Becket at Canterbury. He requested 'a picture of the blessed Thomas the Martyr with the four knights who slew him'.[3] While he stayed at Chester, Edward received his first group of tenants which consisted of five barons, four knights and two clergymen. They each did homage and swore fealty and were required to produce written title to their lands within a fixed time. In the days that followed, other tenants similarly came to acknowledge their new overlord. Edward then went on to Wales, receiving his tenants at the centres of Flint, Hope, Ruthin, Rhuddlan and Conwy. Men came from all over Wales to meet their new overlord and pay their respects. He did not go to Caernarvon, where the castle had been sacked by the rebellious Welsh in 1294. By 1301 parts of it had been rebuilt, but perhaps it was not yet in a suitable state for a royal visit.[4]

In May, Edward travelled to Kenilworth Castle, where he rejoined the King. While he was at Kenilworth, various English lords came to offer homage for their estates in Wales. As Edward travelled around the country, others similarly did homage when they met their overlord. Chroniclers have suggested that the Welsh felt that they had a special relationship with a Prince who had been born among them. 'The King gave the Principality of Wales to his son Edward. This pleased them greatly because he had been born in Wales and held the earldom of Chester'.[5] Certainly, his Welsh tenants sent petitions to the Prince and his advisers at his manor of Kennington, near London. However, the Prince's powers of action were limited and petitioners were told to take their business to the Welsh Justices, or produce written evidence in support of their case. In direct contrast to the rather rosy view of the chroniclers, Edward complained about the rough Welsh people and his lands there. He wrote to Louis, Count of Evreux:

> We send you a big trotting palfrey (a saddle-horse for riding), which can hardly carry its own weight, and some of our bandy-legged harriers (hunting-dogs) from Wales, who can well catch a hare if they find it asleep, and some of our running dogs, which go at a gentle pace; for well we know that you take delight in lazy dogs. And, dear cousin, if you want anything else from our land of Wales, we can send you plenty of wild men if you like, who will know well how to teach breeding to the young heirs or heiresses of great lords.[6]

But while he critcized the people, he enjoyed their music. Gerald of Wales, writing in the thirteenth century, had commented on the musical skills of the Welsh. He said that they had three special musical intruments: the harp, the pipe and the crowd (a forerunner of the violin). He referred to the sweetness of sound and the speed of their fingers as they cleverly changed the rhythms, playing tunes that were seductively soothing.[7] This musical talent was pleasing to the Prince and he sent one of his servants, Richard the Rhymer, to the Benedictine Abbey at Shrewsbury, so that he might stay at the Abbey and learn to play the crowd. There are other references to musicians playing the same instrument for Edward's entertainment and he had yet another crowder who played for him at Windsor.[8]

Following the grant of the Principality, there were changes in the Prince's Household. William of Bliborough, who had previously been Keeper of the Household, now became Chancellor, and Walter Reynolds took Bliborough's place as Keeper and Treasurer to the Prince. Reynolds' accounts for 1301 reveal that Edward had the companionship of ten young men, who were roughly his own age. These were 'high-born youths, attached to the Prince's Household for their education'. Chief among them was Gilbert of Clare, Edward's nephew, who later became Earl of Gloucester. Nine of them each had their own *magister*, or tutor; the only exception was Piers Gavaston, a Gascon by birth. The Prince's Household also included his cousin, Henry Beaumont, who was related to the royal families of both England and France. Close ties of loyalty and friendship between Edward and his young companions endured for many years.[9]

While Edward's acquisition of lands in Wales and Cheshire did not occur until 1301, he already, in name at least, held lands in France. When his mother died in 1290 he inherited the counties of Ponthieu and Montreuil, which lay in north-western France, not far from Boulogne. Because he was only six years old at the time, the lands were held on his behalf by Edmund of Lancaster, brother of the King. In 1294 Ponthieu and Montreuil were taken over by the King of France, in much the same way as he attempted to annex the Duchy of Gascony. However, by the Treaty of Montreuil, the lands were returned to England. Edward I handed over management of these areas to Italian merchants, notably to the family of Frescobaldi of Florence, who were responsible for the administration of the lands and rendered their accounts annually to the Prince's Treasurer.[10]

As Prince of Wales, Edward derived income from the three areas of Cheshire, Wales and the French counties of Ponthieu and Montreuil. At a rough estimate, he was drawing about £1600 from all three. Cheshire was the largest provider of income and, on one occasion, £1000 was sent from Chester to London, packed in baskets, with an escort of 16 men on foot and two on horseback. But income from his lands was not enough to pay the Prince's expenses and additional grants had to be made from the Exchequer and other sources. For example, in 1303. the collectors of a tax on the clergy made an advance of £500 to pay for purchases made in

London for the Prince and his Household, since without such provisions he could not afford to go to the Scottish war.[11]

The King wished to formalize his claim to the throne of Scotland and, on September 26th 1300, he issued writs to various abbots, priors and canons, ordering them to search their chronicles and archives for information concerning entitlement to the Scottish throne and to send it to him. He issued similar orders to the chancellors of the universities of Oxford and Cambridge urging them to send learned men to the next Parliament at Lincoln to discuss his claim. It was not until February 1301, following the meeting of Parliament at Lincoln, that the King eventually sent a letter to the Pope protesting about papal interference in matters between England and Scotland and setting out his claim to the overlordship of Scotland.[12] He then sent out a call to arms, announcing his intention to attack the Scots as soon as the latest truce expired at Whitsun. In his original plan, he summoned all his forces to muster at Berwick on June 24th, but he later changed this strategy and decided to invade Scotland with two armies, one on the east from Berwick, the other on the west, from Carlisle. Leadership of the western attack provided the Prince with his first independent command. The nobles who were chosen to accompany him were a balance of older, experienced, soldiers and younger men, who were closer to him in age. The group of older men included Henry Lacy, Earl of Lincoln, who was then aged fifty and highly experienced in both war and administration, and Richard Fitzalan, Earl of Arundel, also an experienced soldier. The younger men included Ralph Monthermer, Earl of Gloucester, who had married Edward's sister, Joan, the widow of Gilbert of Clare. There were also Thomas, Earl of Lancaster, and his younger brother, Henry, both cousins of the Prince, and Humphrey Bohun, Earl of Hereford, who married Edward's widowed sister, Elizabeth, in 1303.[13] Many others, who were part of the Prince's company, were linked to him because they were his tenants, or were holders of estates that adjoined his lands in Wales and in Cheshire. In addition to these, others were members of the Prince's Household, including the young men who were his day-to-day companions and, in particular, Piers Gavaston. A number of clerks of the Household also travelled with the Prince, since collecting, feeding and moving an army involved a huge amount of administration and record-keeping.[14]

The records of the Household allow us to see the splendour of the Prince's army, in which some of the magnificent warhorses were worth up to £80 each. The lords who travelled with him brought their own equipment and had their own retinues of horsemen and infantry. It is difficult to estimate total numbers, but the Prince's army was large and expensive.[15] His force left Berwick and set out westwards towards Carlisle.

Disappointingly for the Prince, chroniclers suggest that the Scots deliberately avoided any encounters 'Since none of the Scots put up any resistance, they (the King and the Prince) achieved nothing of importance or deserving of praise'.[16] There were a few skirmishes during September, but the season for fighting ended without any decisive action. Because of this, the King decided to stay in the north so that he would be ready to take up the campaign early the following year. He also decided to keep his garrisons in the castles, in case of an attack at any time.[17] A chronicler reported that the Prince was 'in good estate and health' when he arrived at Carlisle, but he may have been ill while staying there, since his doctor left for London in October with orders to fetch 'matters required for the Prince's body' and return as soon as possible.[18] Edward remained at Carlisle until the end of October and on November 14th he reached Linlithgow, about 15 miles west of Edinburgh. Although the Prince had fought no battles with the Scots, he seems to have conducted himself well in the campaign.

One of the chief problems faced by both King and Prince was a shortage of cash to pay their soldiers. A chancery clerk wrote saying that he was sending extra cash to the Prince at Carlisle and to the King at Berwick, hoping that there would be enough to pay their armies. At the same time, he begged the King to make the money last as long as possible, because of the difficulties of keeping the garrisons properly supplied through the winter. The King's force consisted of about 6800 men on foot, accompanied by their officers, and some light horsemen. Most of his troops were archers; with these, there were 20 crossbowmen, 20 masons and 20 miners. The records reflect the importance of engineering equipment for sieges; the King was supplied with 'two good engines, the master engineer and six carpenters'.[19] However, the campaign was quickly abandoned when, on Christmas day in 1301, Philip IV, King of France, issued letters patent confirming a treaty between French and English envoys. As a condition of this treaty, there was to be truce between England and Scotland until St Andrew's day (November 30th) 1302. Edward I also confirmed the treaty and left Scotland. Neither the King nor the Prince of Wales returned to Scotland until May 1303.[20]

By the autumn of 1302 the truce was running out and the question of Scotland was once more under consideration. According to a chronicler 'the whole kingdom advised the King to crush the Scottish rebels, now that the truce was coming to an end'.[21] Preparations were under way in November and December. The Prince spent Christmas at South Warnborough in Hampshire at the house of Sir Roger Pedwardine and, while he was staying there, he bought a present for his stepmother, Queen Margaret, as her New Year's gift. It was a gold ring with a great ruby in it.

In February he went to Langley, which was now his own property, and he entertained the King and Queen there for a week.[22]

The King had planned to reach Berwick by May 1303. However, the Scots were already attacking the English garrisons there and the King speeded up his arrangements. In March, the Prince went to Holborn in London to inspect the work carried out by the royal tentmakers. In all, they made 28 tents and pavilions, providing a complete, but temporary, palace. One of the structures was a great canvas hall; another was a private chamber for the Prince. There were stables, a chapel, a council-chamber, and individual small tents for the members of the Household. All this equipment and vast amounts of other items were loaded on to carts as the forces began to move northwards from London in March 1303. For the first time, sulphur appeared as an item in the accounts, suggesting the use of gunpowder, of which sulphur is a major ingredient. The importance of sulphur lies in its ability to burn at a low temperature and ignite quickly. The use of gunpowder changed the character of siege-warfare, making it much more difficult for defenders to withstand an attack.[23]

The King and the Prince travelled in separate parties. The Prince's Household accounts give details of the items and the people that accompanied him. These included a lion, that travelled in its own cart, in the care of its keeper, Adam of Lichfield. There was Robert of Cisterne, physician to the Prince, who organized medicines, syrups, powders, herbs and ointments 'for the cure of the Household in the war.' The equipment included two urinals encased in leather coffers, for the Prince's use. John, the coppersmith, made a great brass cauldron for the Prince's kitchen in the war, while an iron oven and other cooking equipment was dispatched from London. The Prince had four sets of winter clothes provided by the King and Queen, and summer clothes were bought in June for the Prince and his Household. The accounts also show the lighter side of war, with payments for pastimes such as fowling, falconry and hunting. There was plenty of gambling and the Prince lost money to the Count of Evreux and the Earl of Gloucester. There were water sports in the cold month of February when Edward paid his fool, Robert Buffard, for playing tricks with him, 'in the water'. Music played a part in the entertainment, with minstrels and trumpeters performing on various occasions. Money was given to Janin le Nakare for playing his nakars (kettle-drums) and two Genoese fiddlers, named Bestrude and Beruche, entertained the Prince at Newcastle. The Prince also enjoyed watching wrestling at Tickhill in Yorkshire on his northward journey.[24]

In May, the Treaty of Paris was concluded, which brought peace between England and France. This meant that the English forces could advance northwards without the threat of a French invasion in the south and that France would not be sending help to Scotland. Faced with the prospect of recurrent attacks by the Scots, the King decided to gather his army further west at Roxburgh, instead of at Berwick, as he had originally intended. The advance from Roxburgh began in June and, from then on, the King and Prince travelled widely through Scotland, providing a show of English strength. Only Stirling still remained in Scottish hands. Chroniclers vividly, if inaccurately, described the horrors of a winter in the north, among bears and tigers and the assaults of other wild animals. But the King, 'unafraid of dragons, like a lion, terrified all the animals of the forest'.[25] Descriptions like this reveal the impact of the Scottish wars on the minds of the English who lived in the south of the country. The people of northern England knew the reality; they lived in fear of 'monsters from the north' who so often devastated the land and brought normal life to a halt. 'No services were held in monasteries and churches from Newcastle to Carlisle'.[26]

In spite of such ferocious tales, the Prince stayed in Scotland for the winter and held court at Perth, where he received some of the Scots who had surrendered, including John Comyn. The capture of Stirling Castle remained the final objective. The siege began on April 22nd and lasted for 12 weeks. Once at least, the King almost lost his life but, according to the chronicler, he had a miraculous escape. When he was riding unarmed, he was struck between the legs with a bolt from a crossbow but neither he, nor his horse, was harmed. Although he was frequently in danger, the weapons always fell to the left and right of him, leaving him free of injury.[27] In an effort to take the castle, the King brought up thirteen siege-engines, while the defenders could produce only one, which broke. Eventually, the defenders surrendered, the castle was captured and, as far as the King was concerned, Scotland was conquered. Wallace escaped but he was later captured, taken to London, and executed in 1305. His execution was then regarded as the final act of conquest.[28] As a condition of the Treaty of Paris, Edward I had agreed to go to France to do homage to the French King for his lands there. Instead of travelling in person, he appointed his son as his proxy, with full powers to do fealty to Philip at Amiens, and the Prince travelled to Dover, ready to cross the Channel. However, none of the escorting French noblemen arrived, nor did the letters of safe conduct, so his journey was abandoned and the young Edward spent most of the winter months at Langley.

Prince Edward was now approaching the age of 21. Details about him at this time are revealed in a roll of his letters for the year November 1304 to November 1305. As soon as he was old enough to have his own seal, his clerks would make copies of the letters that were sent out under that seal and the surviving roll contains these copies. By 1304, we can see that his court numbered up to 200 people, headed by his four chief ministers. The most important was the Steward, whose name was not recorded. Secondly, there was Walter Reynolds, who was the Keeper of the Household and concerned with domestic finance; then came the Controller, William of Melton, who was in charge of the Prince's Privy Seal: a responsible task in times of frequent journeys, with the possibility of theft and forgery. Finally, his Chancellor, William of Bliborough, was in charge of the Prince's Great Seal. Below these men in status came knights, squires, clerks and then, on the lowest rungs, the indoor and outdoor servants. Among the knights, there were the young men who were his frequent companions, men like Hugh Audley, Robert Clifford, Hugh Despenser the younger and William Inge, who lent him cash when he overspent or gambled too heavily at dice. He also had two physicians to take care of him, named as Master John of Ludgershall and Robert of Cisterne.

This single roll of letters also gives us details about the Prince's movements during these twelve months. He spent all his time in the southern part of England, staying at Langley for the winter and coming to London only when Parliament was meeting. In the summer months he travelled across the south-east, stopping in Berkshire, at Sonning, White Waltham and at the royal manor-house within the park at Windsor; staying at St Albans in Hertfordshire; at Canterbury, Chartham, Eltham, Sutton-at-Hone and Wye, in Kent; at Edgware, in Middlesex; at Bagshot, Guildford, Kennington, Lambeth and Pirbright, in Surrey; at Battle, Hellingly, Lewes and Midhurst, in Sussex. Hilda Johnstone, who has edited this roll of letters, expressed her disapproval, considering that this limited circuit provided the life of 'a somewhat irresponsible country gentleman, living an uneventful and rather monotonous life'.

However, there was no lack of entertainment for the Prince. The letters reveal his enjoyment of tournaments and his interest in breeding horses and dogs. The first letter on the roll refers to supplies for his squires who were travelling to Berkshire for 'tilts and jousts'. He was interested in buying a stud and he asked his sister Elizabeth to send her white greyhound to mate with one of his, 'for we have a great wish to have puppies from them'. In another letter he asked for a spaniel and a sparrow-hawk, with a trainer for the hawk. As well as indulging material interests, the Prince was a strong supporter of the Dominicans. These men were preaching friars who had become very popular in England during the thirteenth century. The Prince had members of their Order as his confessors and, later on, he set up a Dominican Priory at Langley. His letters show how he intervened on their behalf in Northampton when their new buildings blocked up some of the well-used streets and the local people retaliated by damaging their new cloister and garden. Edward quickly organized Justices to hear the case and punish the offenders. In the same way, he asked the Mayor and citizens of London to allow the Dominicans to build new premises there.[29]

The execution of Wallace in August 1305 appeared to bring Scottish resistance to an end and plans were made to set up a new administrative system for Scotland. The country was to be divided into four, with two Justices (one English and one Scottish) appointed to administer each area. But before a peace-time administration could be put in place, further problems arose. John Comyn, who also laid claim to the throne of Scotland, was murdered at Dumfries in Galloway, and Robert Bruce was crowned King of Scotland at Scone on May 27th 1306. In reply, Edward I began to prepare for yet another invasion and the English forces were called to meet at Carlisle by July 8th. The orders that were issued show that the Prince was intended to play an important part in the venture. It was 'the expedition of Edward, Prince of Wales, to be joined afterwards by the King'.[30]

Before he set out, the Prince, now aged 22, was made a knight in a great ceremony at Westminster. The sheriffs proclaimed throughout the country that any men who wanted to be knighted with the Prince and were entitled to hold that rank, should come to London where they would receive suitable equipment, as a gift from the King.[31] One of the chroniclers described how 300 young men flocked to London to be there at Whitsun for the investiture. So many came that the Palace of Westminster was too small to hold them and many stayed at the New Temple, the headquarters of the Knights Templar that lay near the Thames. Most of the young men kept vigil in the Temple church; just a few were with the Prince at Westminster Abbey. There was great noise and confusion at Westminster; the trumpets and shouts were so loud that the monks could not hear the chants from one side of the choir to the other. In the event, the crowd was so great that war-horses had to be brought in to clear a path to the high altar. In the privacy of the chapel of Westminster Palace, the King knighted his son and created him Duke of Aquitaine. Then, in Westminster Abbey, the Prince knighted the others, including his close friend, Gavaston. The ceremony was followed by a magnificent feast and entertainment.[32] The occasion was also a celebration of the marriage of Eleanor of Clare, the King's granddaughter, to Hugh Despenser the younger, a companion of the Prince. A chronicler extravagantly compared it with the coronation of King Arthur at Caerleon:

Never in Britain, since God was born,
Was there such nobleness in towns nor cities,

Except Caerleon in ancient times
When Sir Arthur the King was crowned there.[33]

The grandeur and excitement of these events were a stimulus to war. On June 8th the Prince went from London to Winchester to visit his stepmother, Queen Margaret, and then left for the north. The King went more slowly, since he was too ill to travel on horseback and, by the time the army was gathering at Carlisle in July, he was still in Nottinghamshire. So, inevitably, the burden of the war fell upon the Prince.

In June, Aymer of Valence, a cousin of the Prince, who later became Earl of Pembroke, met and defeated Bruce at Methven, near Perth. The Prince then led his army to join Valence. On the way northwards through the Annan valley, the Prince's men took Lochmaben Castle, where they waited for supplies to be brought up from Carlisle. Bruce moved into Strathdon for safety and stayed at Kildrummy Castle, which the Prince then besieged. In September he took the castle but failed to capture Bruce who escaped to Kintyre and then, as winter approached, took refuge in the Western Isles. In the meantime, the King reached the Priory of Lanercost in Cumberland, where he stayed for the winter, while the Prince returned to England and spent Christmas at Northampton Castle with his young half-brothers, Thomas and Edmund. Some of the young knights followed the Prince's example and left Scotland but they failed to obtain the King's permission beforehand. Their ill-considered action brought the threat that their estates would be confiscated, but Queen Margaret kindly put in a plea for them. These were young men, friends of the Prince, who were unwilling to spend the winter in Scotland, preferring the excitement of tournaments abroad.[34] In the spring, Bruce and his men led successful attacks against the English forces in Scotland. An English army was again summoned to Carlisle in July, but the King was now very ill. He died at Burgh-by-Sands, not far from Carlisle, on July 7th 1307. His men kept his death a secret until Prince Edward arrived.

The Prince at the time was in southern England, not far from London. News of the King's death reached him on July 11th, although it was another two weeks before written confirmation arrived in London. As soon as he heard the reports, the Prince set off northwards and reached Carlisle on July 18th. Apart from his journey to the north, one of his first actions was to recall Gavaston, who had been recently banished. The Gascon arrived in England early in August and Edward created him Earl of Cornwall on August 6th, perhaps even without Gavaston's knowledge. On his arrival in England, he, too, travelled quickly northwards and, on August 17th, he presided at a banquet at Sanquhar, about 25 miles to the north-east of Dumfries, at which the new King was his guest.[34] The opening lines of Marlowe's play show Gavaston delightedly reading a letter from Edward, inviting him to return to England:

> My father is deceased; come Gavaston, and share the kingdom with thy dearest friend.[35]

The gift of the earldom of Cornwall to a man who was only a knight was an astonishing act: Cornwall was an area that had been extremely profitable to the Crown during the thirteenth century because of the rich deposits of tin and it truly gave Gavaston a share of the kingdom. The earldom was held previously by Edmund, cousin of Edward I and, because of the prestige of the title, Edward I had probably intended to bestow it on one of his younger sons by his second wife, Queen Margaret. In addition to becoming Earl of Cornwall, Gavaston was betrothed to Margaret of Clare, who was the daughter of Joan of Acre and niece of the new King. In this way, the Gascon became a member of the royal family more or less 'by the backdoor'.[36] Chroniclers focused their anger on this Gascon 'retainer'; even before the old King was buried, they depicted Edward and Gavaston looking on while the chests containing the royal jewels were broken open:

> The King then gave him a hundred thousand pounds of silver, as well as gold and precious stones and many jewels. Almost all of which Peter sent by the hands of merchants to his homeland.[37]

Marlowe also emphasized Edward's pleasure at the return of his old friend and his total generosity to him:

> Fear'st thou thy person? Thou shalt have a guard.
> Want's thou gold? go to my treasury.
> Wouldst thou be loved and feared? Receive my seal.[38]

V   PIERS GAVASTON AND THE PRINCE

Many of the problems associated with the early years of the reign of Edward II stemmed from his deep affection for Piers Gavaston. Holinshed, whose chronicle was published in the 1570s, presented the following picture of Gavaston, derived from the *Polychronicon* of Ranulf Higden:

> (Edward) received him into most high favour, creating him Earl of Cornwall and Lord of (The Isle of) Man, his principal secretary and Lord Chamberlain of the realm, through whose company and society he was suddenly so corrupted, that he burst out into most heinous vices; for then using the said Piers as a procurer of his disordered doing, he began to have his nobles in no regard, to set nothing by their instructions and to take small heed unto the good government of the commonwealth.

Holinshed went on to comment on Gavaston's aim of amusing and entertaining Edward, while at the same time piling up offices and honours for his disreputable friends.[1] Marlowe echoed Holinshed's version, emphasising Gavaston's ability to amuse Edward and picturing him as a typical Elizabethan courtier:

> I must have wanton poets, pleasant wits,
> Musicians that, with touching of a string,
> May draw the pliant King which way I please.
> Music and poetry is his delight.[2]

Gavaston was a younger son of Arnaud Gavaston, a landowner in Bearn, a district which lay in the southern part of Gascony. Arnaud Gavaston had fought for Edward I in his campaign in Wales in 1282-3 and was used twice as a hostage by the King on the continent. In 1294-6, while he was held hostage for the second time, he escaped to England. Perhaps his son travelled with him, since Piers was in England in 1296 and went to Flanders in 1297 in the service of Edward I. Piers had little to lose by leaving his homeland, as he had had no lands to inherit and his main chance of advancement lay in gaining the favour of Edward I. He was clearly successful in this; by 1300, he had joined the Household of Edward of Caernarvon and was serving with him in the Scottish campaigns. The name of *Pierotus de Gavaston* appears among the lists of those claiming expenses for the loss of their horses in the Scottish war. During this time, Gavaston rose from being just a squire in royal service to being described as a friend *(socius)* of the Prince. Piers may have been just a few years older than Edward and a close friendship developed between these two men.[3] An anonymous chronicler recorded Edward's strong attachment to Gavaston:

> and when the King's son saw him, he fell so much in love that he entered upon an enduring compact with him, and chose and determined to knit an indissoluble bond of affection with him before all mortals.[4]

In 1304 a dispute arose between the Prince and his father, which caused a temporary separation between Edward and Gavaston. There was a report that the Prince had insulted Walter Langton, Bishop of Coventry and Lichfield, Treasurer of the Exchequer and chief adviser to the King. A quarrel arose possibly because the Prince had broken into some of Langton's woodland.[5] Whatever the cause may have been, the Prince had replied to Langton with insulting words and Langton complained to the King. As a result, the King banished his son from his presence and forbade his officials to provide him with money. Edward complained about his father:

> He is so angry that he has forbidden all the officers of his Household and the Exchequer to give us or lend us anything for the sustenance of our Household. We have remained at Midhurst (Sussex) waiting for his good pleasure and his pardon.

The King had, in fact, travelled through Midhurst on his way to Guildford, but the Prince kept at a respectful distance from his father. The King had found an effective way of putting controls on his son and forced him to reduce the size of his Household and check other expenditure, especially on building work. The Prince was clearly interested in architecture, which is not surprising, since he had probably observed stonemasons and other craftsmen at work on royal houses and castles from early boyhood. He had already begun to increase the number of royal houses, a process which he was to continue in later years. He had ordered work to be carried out on the manor-house at Byfleet, in Surrey, to alter and redecorate it for his use. Carpenters and ditchers were brought in; there were bills for plaster of Paris, for tiles from Flanders and for colours for painting the house.[6] However, such operations were expensive and he was even forced to abandon work at Langley, where he had begun to add extra buildings to the site. Perhaps his father was afraid that the Prince was 'surrounding himself there with undesirable companions'. Fortunately, he was not totally without funds since a few close friends made money available to him, in spite of the King's orders. Above all, his stepmother, Queen Margaret, and his sisters rallied to his support. His sister, Mary, invited him to stay at Amesbury, while Joan lent him her seal because he could not borrow money using his own seal. His lack of money caused the Prince to be concerned about having suitable clothes and horses at a time when members of the French royal family were coming to England and he wrote to Walter Reynolds asking him to provide, 'the best and finest clothes you can find for sale in London, with fur and satin and all things proper for them'. Eventually, the King relented, gradually allowing him money to pay for necessities. The Prince took his revenge later: when he succeeded to the throne, one of his first actions was the dismissal of Langton.[7]

Although his allowances were increased, the Prince was still without many of his friends. He wrote to his sister, Elizabeth, saying that two of his former companions had returned to him, but he asked her to use her influence with Queen Margaret to persuade the King to let him have Gilbert of Clare and Piers Gavaston as part of his Household once more. The Prince wrote:

> If we had those two, along with the others whom we have, we would be greatly relieved of the anguish which we have endured and from which we continue to suffer from one day to the next.[8]

He was pleased when his friends sent him gifts. Hugh Despenser the younger sent him raisins and wine, 'which came at the right time, just as he was going to dinner'. Others gave gifts of greyhounds and other dogs and helped him to buy the stud of horses that had become available following the death of the Earl of Surrey. He wrote from Battle, in Sussex, urging the Earl's executors to 'fix a time, sure and convenient, when our people may examine the stud and fix a price and day to make payment'. He succeeded in taking over the stud and kept it at Ditchling, near Lewes. The quarrel with his father was finally settled by October 1304, when the Prince attended a banquet in the hall of Westminster Palace. If nothing else came of this episode, it showed the Prince who his true friends were: his stepmother, Queen Margaret, his sisters, Elizabeth, Joan and Mary, Piers Gavaston, Gilbert of Clare, Hugh Lacy and Hugh Despenser the younger.[9]

In 1307 another dispute arose between the King and his son, which this time directly involved Gavaston. The King ordered the Gascon to leave the country and stay away until he had permission to return. There are no clear accusations against him, only 'certain reasons' for his removal.[10] Since Gavaston received two months' notice and was allowed to stay in England for the next tournament, the reasons for his banishment did not seem to be particularly serious.[11] The chronicler, Walter of Guisborough, provides a colourful explanation for the King's anger. He suggests that the Prince wanted to help his friend, who had no prospect of inheriting estates, and he sent Langton to make the following request to the King:

'My Lord King, I am sent on behalf of the Prince, your son (although unwillingly, as God lives), to ask in his name for permission to promote this knight Piers Gavaston, to be Count of Ponthieu.' The King angrily replied, 'Who are you to dare to ask such things? As the lord lives, if it were not for fear of God, and because you said at the beginning that you were reluctant to undertake this business, you would not escape my hands. But now, I will see what he who sent you has to say, and you shall not go away.' Having said this, he called for the Prince and asked, 'On what business did you send this man?' The Prince replied, 'So that, with your consent, I could give the county of Ponthieu to Piers Gavaston'. 'You low-born son of a whore', said the King, 'do you want to give your lands away now, you who never gained any? As the Lord lives, if it were not for fear of destroying the kingdom, you would never enjoy your inheritance'. He then seized the Prince's hair in both hands and tore out as much as he could, until he was exhausted and he drove him out.[12]

After this encounter the King held a meeting with his advisers and decided to banish Gavaston. While the chronicler presents a supposedly *verbatim* version of the meeting between the Prince and his father, it may not be very far from the truth. Although Langton was certainly no friend of the Prince, Edward knew that the King would at least listen to a request from his chief adviser. In addition, Ponthieu was in the gift of the Prince, as part of his mother's inheritance, so he was not asking the King to provide Gavaston with a gift of Crown property. In the event, the subterfuge of using Langton to put the request did not succeed and Gavaston was banished. The Prince accompanied him as he travelled to Dover and gave him presents for the journey. These included colourful tapestries, two splendid sets of clothes, suitable for him to wear at tournaments, five horses and a large sum of money. Gavaston's companions also received lavish gifts of money and goods.[13] The Gascon remained in France until the death of Edward I in 1307 gave him the chance to return to England.[14]

The evidence points to a homosexual relationship between these two men. Fourteenth-century chroniclers accepted that there was a deep friendship between them, even to an excessive degree. They described it as 'beyond the bounds of moderation' *(ultra modum)*, referring to 'this unique and excessive love' and Edward's desire for 'wicked and forbidden sex'.[15] The chronicle of Meaux Abbey stated unequivocally that Edward took 'too much delight in sodomy', which suggests that a certain level of indulgence was acceptable, but that he overstepped the limit.[16] Although sodomy was regarded as a hideous crime and was a 'sin against nature', the Church had previously presented a sympathetic and understanding attitude towards homosexuality.[17] Anselm, Archbishop of Canterbury, giving instructions about how to deal with it among the clergy, declared in 1102 that 'up to now, this sin was so common that hardly anyone was ashamed of it and that many people, ignorant of its magnitude, fell headlong into it'. The punishment was excommunication but, factors such as their age and whether they had wives or not, were to be taken into account, all of which suggests that it was a common occurrence and was treated with tolerance. During the second half of the thirteenth century there was a change in attitude towards homosexuals as part of a general trend in hostility towards those who did not conform. In the minds of many, a clear link was apparent between homosexuality and heresy, as deviant behaviour which deserved to be punished. These ideas led to an increase in legislation throughout Europe concerning homosexuality, when laws were directed against laymen as well as the clergy. The severity of punishment was increased; forgiveness by an ordinary confessor was not enough and offences had to be investigated by a Bishop. Some offenders might be punished by burning or castration instead of being fined, but there is no evidence to show that heavier penalties reduced homosexuality.[18] In addition, homosexual activity and the practice of heresy were the most frequent charges brought against the Knights Templar in 1311. But in any all-male communities, where each man was heavily dependent on his companions, strong bonds of friendship and emotion were likely to be formed.[19] Even in such a climate of hostility, if Edward and Gavaston had been prepared to act with greater discretion, their relationship would probably have been accepted. It was their public and open demonstration of affection that aroused so much comment.

Such a close bond between the Prince and Gavaston led Edward to regard the Gascon as his 'brother'. Since all his elder brothers had died as children and John of Brabant had married and left the Household, did

Edward find companionship with his adopted brother, a man whom he felt he could trust totally? Gavaston was a man outside the social hierarchy of the royal circle who had no land or political power. Edward's love for Gavaston may have been based on his personality, as a captivating and exciting newcomer. Against this background, the Prince's eagerness to bestow Ponthieu on his 'brother' may be seen as an attempt to raise him to a level appropriate to his status.[20] While the King did not openly stress the homosexual factor, he probably reacted so violently to the request out of fear that Edward's obsessive attachment to Gavaston would threaten the stability of the kingdom when the Prince inherited it. There is no clear evidence, however, that Gavaston was an evil man, deliberately seeking to influence the Prince. On the contrary, it seemed that it was the Prince's excessive passion for his friend that clouded his judgement. The King's solution was to banish Gavaston from England and so remove him from Edward's company. It may have been during the banishment of Gavaston that the Prince fathered an illegitimate son. About 15 years later, Adam, described as his 'bastard son', was provided with armour and equipment for the Scottish war. There is no indication of who the mother was, but perhaps Edward was required to prove to his father that he was capable of heterosexual acts and could provide an heir to the throne.[21]

VI   THE ACCESSION OF EDWARD II

Edward I had given instructions that his heart should be taken to the Holy Land and his bones should be carried with his army, remaining unburied until the Holy Land was conquered. However, the King's requests were not carried out and his body was slowly brought south. It was brought to Richmond, in Yorkshire, and then lay at the Abbey of the Holy Cross at Waltham, in Essex, from August 14th until October 24th. It was taken to the Priory of Christchurch, near Aldgate in London, then to St Paul's Cathedral. Next day it was carried to Westminster Abbey, where the funeral service took place on October 27th, conducted by Anthony Bek, Bishop of Durham. The King's body was placed in a tomb of Purbeck marble, much plainer than his wife's memorial, and wax candles were kept burning around it for many years afterwards. Edward I had reigned for 35 years; a man of enormously strong character, whose mere physical presence commanded respect. He embodied both contemporary and biblical ideals of kingship, but his son's character was very different.

Edward II inherited the kingdom at the age of 23 and his accession was generally welcomed across the country. He was handsome and endowed with such gifts that made him appear the equal, or even the superior, of other kings. The fourteenth-century author of the *Life of Edward the Second*, declared that, when he began his reign, the omens were good because he was rich and enjoyed the support of his people. He had, in a sense, been well-prepared for his office.[1] He had gained experience of war by serving in various Scottish campaigns; he had acted as regent while his father was absent, and had attended meetings of Parliament. But, in a way that proved to be characteristic of him, he was in no hurry to take up his new role.

Although the chronicler described him as rich, his father's death had left an expensive legacy of payments for the upkeep of castles in Wales, together with the costs of campaigns in Gascony and Scotland and heavy debts to Italian bankers and other individuals. And so the new King was to take up a difficult inheritance when he reached Carlisle on July 18th. He stayed in the north until early September but, by this time, official business was beginning to crowd in on him, so he made sure that the Scottish towns and castles, especially Stirling, Perth and Dumfries, were well-fortified, and he left his cousin, Aymer of Valence (soon to become Earl of Pembroke), to 'guard Scotland'. But Pembroke was quickly replaced by John, Earl of Richmond, who was then left to take command.[2] Edward moved south, sending out orders as he went to the leading men of the northern counties to move into Lancashire, Cumberland and Westmoreland, 'to keep the peace in those lands, to prevent the thievish attacks of Robert Bruce and his accomplices, the King's enemies'.[3] After ordering his falconers to bring trained falcons and hunting-dogs to him at Northampton, Edward then turned his attention to the duties of attending to his father's funeral, arranging his marriage to Isabella of France, organizing the Coronation, and holding a meeting of Parliament.

The first Parliament of his reign was held at Northampton. It granted him income from taxation, which allowed him to pay for his father's funeral and the expenses of the Household. Parliament also confirmed the King's grant of the earldom of Cornwall to Gavaston. Since this was a title that had previously been reserved for members of the royal family, it made Gavaston pre-eminent among the other ten earls. Some of them, particularly Henry Lacy, Earl of Lincoln, supported the grant to Gavaston, but others were opposed to it:

> because Piers was a foreigner, born in Gascony, and because of jealousy. For the magnates of the country loathed him because he alone had the King's favour and ruled like a second King.[4]

Edward aroused further anger by his lavish gifts of gold and silver to Gavaston.[5] Consequently, Edward's great affection for him was outweighed by the hatred of the other lords. The King also granted him the honour and castle of Berkhamsted in Hertfordshire, where the Gascon celebrated his marriage to Margaret of Clare, the King's niece, in great style. To commemorate both the grant of his earldom and his marriage into the royal family, Gavaston arranged a magnificent tournament at Wallingford, in Berkshire. Chroniclers have suggested that he had aroused so much anger and jealousy among the other nobles that none of them would support him and they were all ranged against him. This left Gavaston with the support only of younger, stronger men of less importance, who had more to gain from the encounter. So, not surprisingly, Gavaston's side carried off the spoils of victory, much to the dismay of the nobles.[6]

Shortly after his accession Edward was clearly showing an interest in practical matters. He spent a week at Nottingham Castle and, while he was there, he ordered the constable to begin making alterations in the buildings. These included putting two new chambers in the tower and adding chimneys, privies, doors and windows. The wording of the account suggests that the King supervised the work personally. Certainly, seven out of the 25 carpenters working on the new buildings were part of his usual Household and had come from London with him.[7] The King's interest in practical and mechanical matters stayed with him throughout his reign, perhaps providing him with a means of escape from political pressures.

Gavaston, rightly or wrongly, was regarded as the prime mover in getting rid of Langton, the Treasurer of Edward I, who had already clashed with the new King when he was Prince of Wales. Langton was accused of leaving the Treasury almost empty and he was replaced by Walter Reynolds, who had been Keeper of the Wardrobe to Edward II while he was Prince of Wales. The proceedings against Langton were eventually dropped and he regained his estates but his trial illustrates the financial difficulties of the early years of the new reign, burdened with the costs of the Scottish wars and afflicted with continual shortages of revenue.[8]

Edward spent his first Christmas as King with Gavaston at Wye in Kent, at the manor-house of the Abbot of Battle, and then turned his attention to his marriage to Isabella.[9] A commission, consisting of the Earls of Pembroke and Lincoln, together with the Bishops of Durham and Lincoln, was appointed to conduct the negotiations. These men remained in France until the middle of January 1308, when they returned to Dover to meet the King and escort him to France for the wedding.[10] In a highly controversial move, Edward appointed Gavaston as regent of England during his absence:

> At Dover in the King's chamber at the Priory of St Martin, in the presence of officials, John Langton, Bishop of Chichester, the King's Chancellor, delivered to the King the Great Seal, which he gave to Sir William Melton to be taken with him over the sea, and immediately the King handed over a new seal, recently made in London for the government of the country in the King's absence, in a red bag, to the Chancellor. The Chancellor used them to seal writs under the testimony of Peter de Gavaston, the Keeper of the Realm of England'.[11]

Edward then left for France, where he did homage to Philip IV for the counties of Ponthieu and Montreuil and the English lands in Gascony and married the twelve-year-old Isabella on January 15th 1308 at Boulogne. The widowed Queen Margaret, sister of the King of France, was present at this long-planned union between her stepson and her niece, 'who was one of the fairest ladies in the world'.[12] The King of France gave

Edward some fine war-horses and other splendid gifts which, according to one of the chroniclers, Edward immediately sent to Gavaston.[13] The Gascon's position as regent gave him precedence over all officials and over all other members of the royal family. Although Edward's half-brothers, Thomas and Edmund, were aged only seven and six, it was not unusual for such young children to be made regents, in name at least. In fact, Edward himself had been nominally in command of a military force at the age of 11 in his father's absence. However, it was Gavaston, the King's adopted brother, who was left in charge. Contrary to what might have been expected, the period of his regency passed quietly, nor did he use his position to take advantage of his power. It was, in fact, the King who showed remarkable lack of restraint in making the appointment, since his action aroused a great deal of anger and resentment among the English nobles.[14] Chroniclers were loud in their condemnation of the King; the author of the *Life of Edward II* wrote:

> It was an astonishing thing that a man who had recently been an exile and had been driven out of England, should now be made ruler and guardian of that same land.[15]

The writer of the *Annals of St Paul's* commented on the incomprehensible extent of Gavaston's power:

> But the more virulently people attacked Gavaston, the more keenly the King loved him. Whenever one of the lords required a favour of the King, Edward sent him to Gavaston to arrange it. Whatever Gavaston said or planned, this was done and the King approved. So people said there were two Kings, one in name and one in reality.[16]

Marlowe referred to Gavaston as a 'night-grown mushroom', emphasising his sudden rise to great power, while other writers described him as a man 'raised from the dust' or 'raised from a dung-heap'.[17] This image of Gavaston has dominated the views of the chroniclers; he was seen as a powerful, influential figure, splendid, arrogant and successful because of his friendship with the King but, at the same time, a figure of total evil. He was depicted as a 'despicable favourite' who had so ensnared the King with love that he became the most powerful man in the kingdom. 'From being just a tiny spark of light, he became a blazing star', outshining all the rest. There were references to a homosexual relationship and to the King's desire for 'sinful, forbidden sex'.[18] However, Edward ignored any signs of disapproval and had complete trust in Gavaston, using him as a close and confidential friend and as a deputy to conduct any day-to-day business that did not interest him.

Discontent among the nobles began to surface, even while the King was still at Boulogne for the wedding. In January 1308, the Bishop of Durham, the Earls of Hereford, Lincoln, Pembroke and Surrey and five others who were at Boulogne, drew up letters patent, declaring that, by their act of fealty, they had bound themselves to maintain the honour of the King and the rights of the Crown. They stressed their loyalty to the King and promised to put right every thing that had been done in the past which might have endangered the King's honour and the rights of the Crown. At the same time, they wished to remove the hardships that had been inflicted on the people in the past and were still continuing. There was no direct mention of Gavaston nor any sense of hostility to the King. On the contrary, these men were asserting their loyalty to Edward, but with the aim of initiating much needed reforms within the financial and administrative system, before others might demand stronger action.[19]

VII   THE CORONATION

Edward returned to England after his wedding and began to make arrangements for the Coronation. One of his first acts on his return was to introduce a measure to avert trouble by banning tournaments and jousting at Croydon (Surrey) before the Coronation. Croydon lies within ten miles of London and there was always a chance that a tournament, which was intended to be a social occasion, would develop into an outbreak of violence, since it involved so many armed men. Similar bans on tournaments were a common occurrence throughout the remainder of his reign.[1] Then Edward turned his attention to the practical details of supervising building work at Westminster. A great deal of work had already been carried out at Westminster Palace to make it suitable for the new Queen, as the fire during the reign of Edward I had destroyed the royal apartments. The rebuilding was now completed and the apartments refurnished. Unusually for a man in his position, the new King took a keen interest in the construction work and exercised personal supervision over some of the details. It was on his instructions that an extra room, known as the White Chamber, was built to adjoin the Green Chamber. Also on his orders, another White Chamber was added next to the Painted Chamber and served as his bedroom. The gardens were freshly turfed, the fish-ponds reinstated and the pier, known as 'the Queen's bridge' was repaired. The royal ship 'The Margaret of Westminster' was meanwhile fitted out for Isabella, under the close supervision of the King. The records of the work illustrate Edward's interest in things of a practical and mechanical nature.

As well as making permanent additions to the Palace, workmen constructed temporary buildings for the Coronation. They put up a great timber hall, specially built for the King's enthronement, and 14 smaller halls to accommodate the guests. 40 ovens were built to cook the Coronation banquet and any empty spaces in Westminster Palace were crammed with extra tables and benches. Set in the middle of the structures was an ingenious device composed of lead pipes and other pieces of equipment that formed a fountain, flowing with wine, both red and white and spiced. 1000 tons of good wine had been ordered for the Coronation from Gascony and Bordeaux, paid for by Italian merchants, the Frescobaldi family of Florence. The ale came from London merchants who also supplied 'large cattle, boars, wood, coal and large and small fish', and lampreys were brought from Gloucester. John le Discher of London provided plates, dishes and salt-cellars, while others made armour, beds and clothes for the King. Roger Frowick, the goldsmith, received £20 for repairing the royal sceptre.[2] All the English nobles were summoned to Westminster Abbey for the ceremony, while other guests came from abroad, including relations of the Queen from France and Edward's sister, Margaret, and her husband, now the Duke and Duchess of Brabant.[3]

In spite of all the elaborate preparations, the ceremony was postponed for about a week. The reason for the postponement is not clear. One writer implied that the nobles were demanding the banishment of Gavaston and the crisis was averted only when the King promised that he would comply with their demands at the next meeting of Parliament, a promise he later disregarded. Others suggested that the delay was caused by the absence of Robert Winchelsey, Archbishop of Canterbury, who was in France and in poor health at the time. Edward wrote to Winchelsey, urging him to return for the Coronation, but he failed to attend and his place was taken by the Bishop of Winchester.[4] The ceremony eventually took place on February 25th 1308. At the Coronation it was traditional for nobles to carry various items of Edward the Confessor's regalia in the procession. Such items included the cross, the crown, the sceptre, spurs and sword. The description of Edward's procession goes as follows:

On Sunday next after the Feast of St Peter in Cathedra (February 25th), Sir Edward, son of King Edward, was crowned in the church of St Peter, Westminster, before the great altar, by Henry, Bishop of Winchester (Robert, Archbishop of Canterbury, being beyond the sea). The prelates, earls and other nobles carried the regal insignia: William Mareschall the great gilt spurs, the Earl of Hereford the royal sceptre, Henry of Lancaster the royal rod. Then came the Earls of Lancaster, Lincoln and Warwick, carrying three swords, and the sword called *Curtana* was carried by the Earl of Lancaster. The Earl of Arundel, Thomas de Vere, son of the Earl of Oxford, Hugh Despenser and Roger Mortimer of Wigmore carried royal vestments. The King's Treasurer followed, carrying the paten of the chalice of St Edward, then the King's Chancellor with the chalice itself. Then came Peter de Gavaston, Earl of Cornwall, carrying the royal crown. Then followed the King.[5]

The lords were outraged to discover that Gavaston was taking such a leading role. He carried the crown of Edward the Confessor and walked immediately in front of the King. He also fastened the gilt spur to the

King's left foot, which placed him next in precedence to Charles, Count of Valois, brother of the King of France, who fastened the right spur.[6] After the consecration, Gavaston carried one of the swords of state, the *Curtana*, or blunted sword of mercy, which the Earl of Lancaster had carried in the procession. All this placed Gavaston firmly in the centre of events, as if he really were the brother of the King, taking precedence over the English nobles.[7] Gavaston's ostentatious dress also aroused plenty of comment. While others wore clothes decorated with gold, his were purple and embroidered with pearls, outshining even the King. His extravagance led to charges that he had ransacked the Treasury and unjustly confiscated peoples' lands and property to support his lavish tastes.[8] In spite of the elaborate preparations, there was a certain amount of confusion at the Coronation because of the numbers of people present. One of the walls near the high altar collapsed and crushed a knight who happened to be standing there. Because of the uproar, the Coronation was carried out 'with excessive haste and in a disrespectful manner'. The banquet, too, was badly managed, since nobody seemed to be in charge.[9] The Coronation also highlighted the general dislike of Gavaston:

> A certain foreigner, from Gascony, called Peter of Gavaston, aroused the hatred of nearly all the great lords of England, because the new King loved him excessively and irrationally, and supported him totally.[10]

The Queen's relations were equally upset, believing that Edward was more in love with Gavaston than with his new wife, whom he treated with contempt, and they returned to France in a state of rage. Again a chronicler stressed the influence of Gavaston and described the King's obsession:

> The mad folly of the King of England, rejected by God and men, who was so overcome with his own wickedness and desire for sinful, forbidden sex, that he banished his royal wife and her sweet embraces from his side.[11]

The King took his Coronation oath in French rather than in Latin, as his ancestors had done, probably because French was the common language of the people who were present. Unlike his immediate ancestors, who made three promises, his oath had four components. He swore to continue the laws and customs that previous Kings had granted; to maintain peace; to do justice; and finally, to keep 'the rightful laws and customs which the community of the realm shall have chosen'.[12] This fourth promise was vague, but it may have been worded in such a way that it would commit the King to support the decisions of Parliament, 'the community of the realm'.

VIII   THE EARLY YEARS OF THE REIGN

The Coronation clearly emphasized the importance of Gavaston to all who were present. There was no doubt that he was the esteemed royal 'favourite'. To the English nobles, he was an upstart Gascon, with a biting wit, who called them by insulting nicknames. For example, he called Thomas, Earl of Lancaster, 'a fiddle-player'; the Earl of Pembroke was 'Joseph the Jew' because of his pale complexion, the Earl of Gloucester was 'a cuckold's bird' and the Earl of Warwick was 'a black dog' because he was dark.[1] Gavaston's attitude increased the resentment of the nobles and, led by the Earl of Lincoln, they made their protests at the Parliament that followed the Coronation. In a session that began on February 27th 1308 and lasted, with interruptions, until after Easter, they set out their grievances. Under the fourth part of the coronation oath, which stated that the King should uphold decisions made by 'the community of the realm', namely Parliament, they presented three chief complaints. They asserted that Gavaston had committed treason by alienating the King from his lords, that he was disinheriting the Crown by taking possession of Crown lands, such as the earldom of Cornwall, and that he was binding his associates to him by oaths.[2] Only the King, Hugh Despenser and John, Earl of Richmond, supported Gavaston. Gilbert of Clare, Earl of Gloucester, refused to take sides; if he supported Gavaston, he would anger the other nobles, if he opposed Gavaston, he would offend the King, who was his close friend and brother-in-law. The other lords swore to deprive Gavaston of his earldom and drive him from the country, arguing that they were showing loyalty to the Crown and were keen to act against anyone who weakened its authority. As the King tried to defend his friend and challenged the right of the nobles to assert such power, he faced the prospect of civil war.[3]

During March 1308 Edward began preparing for war. He dismissed the keepers of various castles, ranging across the country from St Briavels in Gloucestershire in the west, to the Tower of London in the east and to Scarborough in Yorkshire in the north, and put in his own men. On the other hand, Gavaston's enemies had the support of Philip, King of France, and his sister, Margaret, the widow of Edward I. Queen Isabella also joined the attack on Gavaston, writing to her father complaining that her husband was neglecting her. She referred to herself as 'the most wretched of wives' and she saw Gavaston as the cause of her troubles, since he drew the King away from her.[4] Philip had lately inflicted terrible punishments on the Templars, based on charges of heresy and homosexuality. The French King's attitude towards the Templars perhaps reflected his feelings about the close friendship between Edward and Gavaston, which he saw as a dangerous threat to the influence of his daughter, and he may have given money to the Earls of Lincoln and Pembroke to encourage them in their opposition.[5]

There was general fear of what might come. Walter Stapledon, Bishop-elect of Exeter wrote to the English Cardinal, Thomas Joce, saying, 'very evil are the times in England now; and there are many who fear that worse times are still in store for us'.[6] When Edward was eventually faced with armed intervention by the nobles in Parliament, he reluctantly agreed that Gavaston should give up his earldom and go into exile. Furthermore, Archbishop Winchelsey threatened to excommunicate the Gascon if he failed to leave the country by June 25th. In fact, he was excommunicated on the grounds that he caused dissension throughout the country and was a threat to peace and good order.[7]

However, the King cushioned the blow by providing Gavaston with generous grants of property to compensate for the loss of his earldom. While staying at Langley, he bestowed on Piers and Margaret Gavaston castles and lands at Knaresborough and Skipton, in Yorkshire, the castle and lands at High Peak, Derbyshire, where the lead mines were highly productive and profitable, and Carisbrooke Castle on the Isle of Wight.[8] In addition to these grants, Edward also rewarded him with the post of Governor of Ireland, together with all the income from that country. In an unexpected manouevre, the King had bestowed the governorship of Ireland upon Richard Burgh, Earl of Ulster, on June 15th. The next day, the same post was granted to Gavaston, but with increased powers. Perhaps the King wanted to ensure that if his appointment of Gavaston failed, Ulster would be ready to take control. In the event, an alliance was formed between Ulster and Gavaston when Ulster's daughter, Maud, married Gilbert of Clare, who was now Gavaston's brother-in-law.[9] The King stayed close to his friend and accompanied him as far as Bristol, from where he sailed on June 28th with a great retinue, three days after his sentence of excommunication had come into effect.[10] Although they had succeeded in removing Gavaston, the lords felt they had been outwitted, since the hated Gascon was now ruler of Ireland, with all that country's wealth at his disposal.[11] In reality, his year of command in Ireland showed that he was a highly successful and competent military governor.[12]

Even before Gavaston's departure, the King was making plans to bring him back by making concessions to powerful individuals to gain their support. By May 9th he had already prepared the way by granting to his cousin, Thomas of Lancaster, the honorary office of steward of England. Lancaster had notably avoided joining with the other nobles in opposing Gavaston and Edward felt that he now had the chance to ensure Lancaster's support. In a further move to divide the opposition and win over Archbishop Winchelsey to his side, Edward ordered Amerigo dei Frescobaldi, the Italian financier, to withdraw from minting money in Canterbury, allowing the Archbishop to take revenues from the mints.[13] Other similar acts of conciliation followed. For instance, Henry Percy was allowed to take control of Scarborough Castle, which the King had earlier appropriated. To Queen Isabella, Edward granted the counties of Ponthieu and Montreuil to provide her with income for her personal expenses.[14] It was ironic that these gifts now flowed directly from the King whereas, while Gavaston was in the seat of power, such acts of patronage had come from him; his absence only emphasized the extent of his former influence.

Certainly, Gavaston's exile brought about a brief reconciliation between Edward and his nobles. This period of calm encouraged Edward to organize a campaign to restore his friend. He wrote to Philip IV, asking him for help in settling his problems. He also wrote to Pope Clement V and to various Cardinals with similar requests, appealing to them to annul the sentence of excommunication against Gavaston. The King was so successful in his work of conciliation that, in March 1309, the Earls of Pembroke and Richmond, accompanied by the Bishops of Norwich and Worcester, went to Avignon to ask the Pope to reverse Winchelsey's excommunication of Gavaston. Clearly, Edward worked energetically to bring about his friend's return and, even in his absence, he gave Gavaston further grants of property in Gascony, while keeping a watchful eye on his English estates and ensuring that his debts were paid.[15]

In April 1309 Parliament produced a list of grievances which had arisen from the financial problems of the last years of the reign of Edward I. Constant wars, political and economic commitments in Ireland, Gascony and Flanders had left the country with huge financial burdens. When heavy taxation failed to bring in enough money to cover expenditure, Edward I had relied on foreign merchants and bankers to provide him with temporary loans of cash. This left his son with massive debts, with the prospect of more taxation for the country.[16] As a condition for agreeing to new taxes, the nobles asked for reforms to be carried out and for *Magna Carta* to be re-implemented. The King was now in a position to offer these concessions, but only in return for the restitution of lands and honours to Gavaston. He had also obtained absolution for Gavaston from the Pope, on the grounds that the dispute between the King and his nobles had been settled.[17]

The *Statute of Stamford*, issued in July 1309, resulted from these various negotiations. Edward conceded to the demands of the nobles, on condition that Gavaston might return.[18] But the King pre-empted the statute and Gavaston was already in England by June. Edward met him at Chester and a chronicler recorded the King's delight 'as one who receives a friend returning from a long pilgrimage'.[19] Gavaston was reinstated as Earl of Cornwall and the two men spent much time together. For a while they remained in the north, staying at York. In an anonymous letter among the Scottish State Papers, a clerk recorded that Edward, Isabella and Gavaston left York on November 17th and began their journey to the south.[20] Gavaston stayed with the King at Langley for Christmas and the two men passed the time in close companionship *(in mutua conversatione)*. This idyllic Christmas together did not please the nobles, who decided to appear armed at the next meeting of Parliament, on the grounds that the King was entertaining their enemy and they felt threatened by this. In reply, the King, on the advice of his friends, sent Gavaston away to a 'very safe place'.[21] When Parliament eventually met, the nobles presented their grievances to the King. In particular, they complained that the state of the kingdom had worsened since the death of Edward I. They asked for 12 men to be appointed, to be called the Ordainers, who would have the power to issue Ordinances to put things right.[22]

The King was suspicious of the proposals, but he was forced to accept the Ordainers, who were chosen from the most powerful men in the country. 21 were chosen, not 12, as first proposed. These were: the Archbishop of Canterbury, six Bishops–of London, Salisbury, Chichester, Norwich, St David's, and Llandaff; eight Earls–Lincoln, Pembroke, Gloucester, Lancaster, Hereford, Richmond, Warwick, and Arundel; six Barons–Hugh de Vere, Robert Clifford, Hugh Courtenay, John Grey, William Marshall, and William Martin.[23] The list excluded men who were directly dependent on the King for advancement, but it included a number of those who had once been ministers of Edward I, suggesting a desire to return to the ways of the previous reign. The Ordainers began their work in March 1310, even before the King had given his consent to their appointment. It took them about 18 months to complete their task and the Ordinances were submitted to Parliament in August 1311.[24]

The nobles, led by Archbishop Winchesley, had been forced to take a stand against the King, since they found it extremely difficult to co-operate with him. The register of the Archbishop helps to illustrate the problems that any negotiators faced when trying to work with the King.

For instance, Winchelsey had attempted to have a meeting with him at the end of February to deal with a letter from Pope Clement V. The Archbishop waited at Westminster, together with various noblemen, ready to discuss the contents of the letter, which had been written in both French and Latin to make discussion easier. Because the King said he wanted time to think about it, the meeting was postponed until March 15th. Winchelsey stayed at Westminster all that time and then made requests for an answer. At last, the King sent his confessor, a Dominican, to say that he could not give an answer. Finally, at the end of March, the King replied, saying that, to prevent any argument he would reply personally to the Pope.[25] It was characteristic of Edward that he saw no urgency in such matters and would not be forced into making decisions.

IX   EDWARD II IN SCOTLAND

While the Ordainers were busy in London, Edward returned to Scotland. He had abandoned his father's last campaign in 1307, although he had made the Borders safe for the following winter. His failure to follow up his father's work had given Robert Bruce the chance to establish a power base there. He had taken advantage of the lull to defeat his Scottish rivals, men such as Earl William of Ross, John of Lorne and Alexander Macdougall, both of Argyll, who might otherwise have been useful to Edward. The King's failure to implement his father's policy had also angered the Earls of Pembroke and Hereford, whose Scottish estates then came under threat.[1] But eventually, in September 1310, the King proposed a new campaign against Bruce and forces were called to muster at Berwick in the following summer. Noticeably, some prominent lords chose not to accompany the King. Of these, the Earl of Lincoln was made regent; and the Earl of Warwick and several others were among the Ordainers and felt that they were too busy to go to Scotland. Others, such as the Earls of Lancaster, Pembroke and Hereford, hated Gavaston so deeply that they refused to go on a campaign with him. That left the King with the company of the Earls of Gloucester and Surrey and Gavaston.[2] Various lesser lords and knights joined the array: for example, Hugh Audley travelled with a force from Montgomery in Wales to command the town of Roxburgh and both Roger Mortimer and Henry Percy collected large retinues and set out for Scotland.[3] Edward also sent orders to the Earl of Ulster to captain the Irish troops who were about to set out for the Scottish war. But, according to a chronicler, the King's heart was not in the campaign; he was choosing to invade Scotland to avoid the summons of the King of France to do fealty for his lands there. There were rumours that he was frightened to go to France and leave Gavaston in England, in case his friend was killed in his absence.[4] Edward, accompanied by Isabella and Gavaston, then set out for Scotland and spent the winter in the north, setting up court at Berwick. To the dismay of the Ordainers, the King also moved his officials from London; he established the Exchequer at York and ordered his Chancellor, Walter Reynolds, to meet him at Newcastle on December 1st 1310.

The Scottish campaign was not particularly effective and Gavaston achieved the only recorded successes by reaching Perth and ravaging the countryside north of Edinburgh, as far as the Grampian mountains. However, the war gave the King a temporary relief from his political problems. His Wardrobe accounts give details of his first winter in Scotland as monarch. The rivers and ports of the east coast of England were busy providing ships and supplies for the winter campaign. Ships from Sandwich, London, Great Yarmouth, King's Lynn, Grimsby, Kingston-upon-Hull and Hartlepool, carried supplies, weapons and personnel to Newcastle and Berwick. The royal court at Berwick and various other towns and castles were supplied with wine, coal and food, including flour, malt, barley, peas and beans. Casks had to be specially made to store the food and prevent it from rotting in the damp, wintry weather. The shortage of mills in Scotland caused difficulties for the English, since grain had to be taken to Newcastle to be ground and then transferred as flour to the other towns. Fish, especially herring and salmon, was bought from local merchants in Newcastle and Berwick, while German merchants supplied the court with sturgeon.[5]

Some military supplies and engineers were also brought by sea, particularly crossbows and crossbowmen. Robert of Glasham, the King's engineer and master carpenter, played an important part in the campaign. He was responsible for building and maintaining the King's siege-engines (*springaldi*), which were kept at Berwick, Dundee, Roxburgh and Stirling. Artillerymen, stonemasons, carpenters, sawyers, smiths and sappers were also engaged in the campaign. While military matters were of prime concern, the King and his court also found time for diversions such as hunting, music and gambling. The King's falcons were brought from London, and his musicians and artists travelled with the court. Although most resources were concentrated on the Scottish campaign at this time, the King took care to ensure that his southern castles were protected. Those at Windsor and Odiham (Hampshire) were supplied with additional armaments and food, while York and Scarborough were similarly strengthened.[6]

When the Earl of Lincoln, regent of England, died in February 1311, the King replaced him with his own nephew, Gilbert of Clare, Earl of Gloucester, who was nineteen years old at the time. The death of Lincoln was a double blow to Edward; on the one hand, he lost a most loyal supporter and, on the other hand, Thomas, Earl of Lancaster, who had now become one of Gavaston's chief critics, had further increased his wealth and power by acquiring the earldoms of Lincoln, Derby, Leicester, and Salisbury, through his marriage to Lincoln's daughter and heiress, Alice. In the meantime, the King was faced with increasing money problems and he was already borrowing cash from Lincoln's executors, offering some of the crown jewels as security. By June 1311, all the customs dues that had been paid since Whitsun were called in to the Treasury, but none of this was enough for the King's needs and he was forced to call a meeting of Parliament to gain agreement to raise more money.[7] First, he made sure that Gavaston was comfortably lodged in a secure place at Bamburgh Castle, a spectacular defensive position which still dominates the Northumberland coastline, then he slowly moved southwards. He reached London, where he stayed at the house of the Dominicans at Blackfriars. When some of the nobles were late in coming to the meeting, Edward, in characteristic fashion, delayed matters still further by going on a pilgrimage to Canterbury and was several days late for the meeting at Westminster.

X ORDINANCES 1311

The parliamentary session took place during August and September 1311. During this time, Edward tried to protect his friend by agreeing to all the measures that the Ordainers asked for, as long as Gavaston was safe. But they refused to accept his conditions and civil war threatened once more. The King's advisers reminded him of the dangers of civil war, recalling the battles fought by the King's grandfather, Henry III, against Simon de Montfort, Earl of Leicester. Faced with the threat of violence, Edward gave way and agreed to the demands of the Ordainers.

There were 41 points, the result of work on the Ordinances over the previous 18 months. The contents show the determination of the nobles to exert control over the King and, to achieve this, they attempted to get rid of those people in the Household who were thought to have undue influence over him. Their prime target was Gavaston and the charges against him were long and various. Condemnation of him resounds through the statutes as they charged him with 'lording it over the State of the King and of the Crown, gathering to himself all the Treasure of the King, being an open enemy of the King and encouraging evildoers to act worse'. The Ordainers accused him of using his position to remove good men from royal service and replace them with his own friends and supporters. They charged him with using his powers of persuasion to influence the King into evil ways. They said that he had taken all the royal treasure and sent it to Ireland and Gascony; that he had usurped royal power and taken royal lands for his own use and for his supporters; that he had taken blank charters, already sealed with the Great Seal, to use as he wished. In making their charges, they were attacking an arrogant man who had used his close relationship with the King to amass great riches and power, while excluding the nobles from government. In their eyes, Gavaston's influence over the King was responsible for the misfortunes of the kingdom and their jealousy led them to believe that once Gavaston had gone, things would improve. The Ordainers also expressed their hostility to three others who were closely connected with Gavaston. These were: Henry Beaumont, who had been a member Edward's Household when he was Prince of Wales, and had received substantial grants of lands and manors, including the Isle of Man; Isabella de Vescy, Beaumont's sister, who held Bamburgh Castle; and the Italian banker, Amerigo dei Frescobaldi. They suspected that Gavaston was using his connections with Italian and Gascon bankers to move money out of England and that the King was placing himself at the mercy of foreign bankers by his heavy borrowing.[1]

The Ordainers hoped to control the King by controlling the royal finances, arguing that revenues should be paid directly to the Exchequer and that the King's expenses should be met out of Exchequer funds. They forbade prises (the requisitioning of goods for the use of the King) against the wishes of the owner and without proper payment and abolished new customs dues levied since the Coronation of Edward I. By abolishing these customs and preventing the King borrowing money from foreign bankers, they left him in an impossible financial situation. They tried to impose further restraints on him, forbidding him to leave the country, or to make war, or to appoint a regent, without the consent of Parliament. They also wished to control the appointment of his chief officers and they restricted the use of his Privy Seal, which he used in his private correspondence, on the grounds that letters sent under the Privy Seal might conflict with the law of the land. To secure their control over the Household, they demanded that a clerk should become Keeper of the Privy Seal, and they asked for meetings of Parliament to be held regularly, once or twice a year. They seemed to think that, without the evil influence of Gavaston, the King could be kept under control and so they ordered the Gascon to be sent away into exile once more and to leave from Dover by November 1st 1311. He was forbidden to live in any part of the King's lands, which covered England, Wales, Ireland, Gascony and Ponthieu. In fact the *Annals of London* suggest that he left on November 3rd and not from Dover, but from London, sailing across the Channel and probably landing on the coast of northern France.[2]

Ostensibly, all this was agreed by the King, who accepted the terms and confirmed them. The Ordinances were then proclaimed in London, 'at the stone cross in the great cemetery at St Paul's, in the presence of the Archbishop and the Earls of Lancaster, Hereford, Pembroke, Warwick and others'. Copies of the document, issued under the King's Great Seal, were sent to every county and placed in every cathedral. Lancaster later put up a plaque at St Paul's to commemorate the Ordinances and emphasize the King's acceptance.[3]

The King's reaction to the Ordinances was predictable. He was furiously angry, declaring that he was being treated like an idiot who was incapable of managing his own affairs. Straightaway, he set about organizing Gavaston's return.[4] However, the Ordainers found that it was one thing to issue Ordinances and quite a different thing to put them into practice. In fact, the Ordinances were often re-issued but never fully implemented, and they were eventually repealed in 1322. The sweeping changes that the Ordainers had envisaged never took place.[5]

XI   THE TEMPLARS

Gavaston's enemies, as previously mentioned, had the support of Philip IV, King of France, perhaps arising from his obvious hostility towards the Templars.[1] Philip had persuaded Pope Clement V to grant him the power to destroy the Templars in France. The Order of the Temple was a military and religious organization that originated after the Christian conquests in the Holy Land during the early twelfth century. It was set up to protect pilgrims as they travelled to the holy places and the Templars took their name from their headquarters in Jerusalem, which were near the site of the former Temple of Solomon. The Knights Templar took vows of poverty, chastity and obedience and were attached to a religious order, first to the Augustinians and later to the Cistercians; in effect, they were both monks and soldiers. In the eastern Mediterranean their function was chiefly military and they played an important part in the crusades. In Europe they lived like ordinary monks and occasionally women were allowed to join the Order. They, and other military orders like the Hospitallers, formed part of the religious establishment. The Templars were well-regarded in England and attracted many donations of money and property. However, with the capture of the town of Acre by the Mamluks in 1291, the Order lost its base. This had been the last Christian stronghold in the Holy Land and the Templars were accused of failing to carry out their military duties and concentrating too much effort on the accumulation and management of wealth and property. Even before the fall of Acre, there had been moves to amalgamate the military orders in the East. The French King took notice of the charges of heresy and homosexuality that were brought against the Templars and saw the advantage of increasing his income by confiscating Templar property, while destroying heresy at the same time. On his orders, the Knights Templar in France were put in prison on charges of heresy and evil practices and more than 300 of them were burned.[2] The compiler of the fourteenth-century portion of the Lanercost chronicle gave his version of the events in France:

> The Master of the Order of Templars, with many brethren of his Order, publicly confessed, as was said, before my Lord, the King of France, and the clergy and the people, that for 60 years or more, he

and his brethren had performed mock worship before a statue of a certain brother of the Order, and had trodden the image of the Crucified One under foot, spitting on its face, and they had habitually committed sodomy among themselves, and had perpetrated many other iniquities against the faith. On account of which, all the Templars in France were apprehended and imprisoned and their goods were confiscated.[3]

In 1310 the Pope issued a bull condemning the Templars for heresy, for the worship of idols and for sodomy. He was reported as saying that if he could not destroy the Order of the Temple, he would destroy its name and habit and hand over its property to the Knights Hospitallers.[4]

Meanwhile Edward II had become involved in taking action against the Templars in England because he had requested the help of Pope Clement in gaining absolution for the excommunication of Gavaston, which would allow the Gascon to return safely to England. As his part of the bargain, Edward had agreed to dissolve the Order in England. He proceeded with less enthusiasm than the King of France but, as with Philip, his action brought him a useful financial advantage. Although the Pope nominally retained control of Templar property, the confiscation of so much land and wealth gave Edward extensive powers of patronage in the redistribution of Templar assets. Before this time, there had been no expressed hostility towards the English Templars. On the contrary, Sir Brian Jay, Master of the Temple, had been the only knight to be killed in Edward I's army at the Battle of Falkirk in 1298 and the Treasurer of the Temple had raised money for the Scottish campaigns in 1303.[5] In addition, the Templars had frequently acted for the Crown as financial administrators, while the Templar buildings in London had been used during the knighting ceremony of the Prince of Wales in 1306.

However, once the initiative had been taken against the Templars, hostility towards them quickly spread. The first orders went out in December 1307 when all the sheriffs throughout England, Wales, Scotland and Ireland were commanded to arrest all members of the Order within their areas of jurisdiction. The Templars were not to be harshly treated, as if they were criminals; on the contrary, the sheriffs were told to guard them 'but not in a hard and vile prison, and to find them sustenance'. Inventories of Templar property were also to be made.[6] The Templars were collected in three major centres in England: at the Tower of London and the castles of Lincoln and York, while those in Ireland were taken to Dublin. Any who attempted to evade capture by giving up their vocation were also to be arrested. Revenue from the Templar property was to be used to provide upkeep for those in prison, at the rate of 4d a day each. Because of the large numbers of Templars in and around London, it was difficult to find accommodation for them all and they had to be housed in the gatehouses of London and in any 'convenient places'. Although the first orders against the Templars had gone out in 1307, it was two years before an opening meeting of senior churchmen was called at St Paul's Cathedral to organize enquiries about individuals. Eventually, the former Templars were dispersed to abbeys and religious houses throughout the country.[7]

The *Annals of London* recorded the accusations against them in 1311. They stated that the Templars contracted homosexual marriage; they were totally obedient to the Grand Master; they denied Christ; they spat and urinated on the Cross; they believed that men were like animals and had no souls after death. They wore the symbol of the Cross on their clothes opposite the anus, so that they sat on it. They did not need to make confession to a priest, but could be absolved by the Grand Master or a layman. They gave the sacrament to those who had been excommunicated. On admission, they were given the 'foul kiss', between the person admitted and the one admitting him, this was a kiss on the mouth, the navel, the anus and the back, sometimes on the genitals. One said he had his eyes covered and did not know where he kissed the other brother. They committed sexual acts with one another and worshipped idols, principally a 'golden head'. Those who did not wish to take part in such rituals were killed or imprisoned, while those who joined were sworn to secrecy under threat of death or imprisonment.[8] The absolute secrecy of the Order gave momentum to all kinds of rumours and partly contributed to its downfall. Edward II officially took action against the Templars in 1307, but he was slow to hand over their property to the Hospitallers. In this way, he provided himself with an extensive 'windfall', which allowed him to be less directly dependent on the will of Parliament for money. The Pope pronounced the end of the Order in 1312.[9]

XII   THE RETURN OF GAVASTON

The nobles had got rid of Gavaston once more, but only for a short time. He left England on November 3rd 1311 but he was unwelcome in France because of the hostility of Philip IV and he moved through Flanders, returning to England at about Christmas.[1] Once again, the King treated the views of the Ordainers with total contempt in his desire to protect Gavaston. Their demands infuriated him and he considered that he was being treated as if he were mad and unable to manage his own affairs. He also resented their interference in the composition of the Household. In anger, he began to reassert his royal powers, first regaining the Great Seal, which had been taken from him. The King and Queen spent Christmas at Westminster but, shortly afterwards, the royal party, consisting of the King and Queen and Gavaston and his wife, moved to York, which had been especially fortified the previous year. Edward used his seal to protect Gavaston and issued writs to the sheriff of York and all other sheriffs proclaiming that Gavaston, who had been exiled, 'contrary to law and custom', had returned to England by the King's order and was 'ready to justify himself before the King, wherefore the King holds him good and loyal'. Edward himself supervised the drawing up of the documents, 'and he took the writs as soon as they were sealed, and put them on his bed'.[2] In a further series of writs, the King granted Gavaston all his former lands and castles. The King also ordered the Chancery officials to join him in York and, by the end of January, the Chancery was established there, at St Mary's Abbey. In effect, the King had his own centre of government at York, where he felt he was safe and among friends, whom he rewarded with generous favours and grants.[3]

The Queen frequently accompanied her husband on his travels and was with him in York at this time. At this date she had an entourage of about 150 attendants, headed by Eleanor Despenser, wife of Hugh Despenser the younger. Eleanor was the elder sister of Margaret Gavaston and both were the sisters of Gilbert of Clare. Among the Queen's ladies were Alice Leygrave, who had once been the King's nurse, and her daughter, Cecilia. The Queen's immediate gentlemen attendants included her physician, Master Theobald, her chaplain, Master Thomas Buchard, and John, her confessor. Peter of Montpelier, who was the King's apothecary, prepared medicines for her, using fenugreek, tragacanth, cloves, cardamom, spikenard, cinnamon and nutmegs as ingredients. Her tailor, John of Falaise, paid 50 workmen for stitching her clothes, which included 15 robes, 30 pairs of stockings, 36 pairs of shoes, three cloaks, six hoods and six bodices. Isabella had a special cloak made for the Feast of Purification (February 2nd), which was decorated with 50 'gold knots', while 500 silver-gilt knots were made for the cloaks of several other robes. There were bills for mending the garments she used when taking a bath and an allowance of 30 pounds of candles for those who made her clothes as they worked by night in winter. Special cases and boxes were made to carry her belongings on her travels and her extensive luggage included her bed. The Queen may have shared her husband's interest in hunting and, like other women of high status, she kept falcons and hunting dogs. She sometimes joined the King and his friends at gambling and lost. The Queen enjoyed music and also had her own jester, named Michael, to entertain her. During her travels she had adopted a Scottish orphan boy, called Thomelinus, to whom she gave food and clothes, and she paid for him to go to London to stay with Agnes, the wife of a French organist, to learn his letters from her. Isabella provided money for the boy's keep and, on one occasion, she paid for 'getting rid of the sores from his head'.[4]

Gavaston may have risked returning to England so soon after his banishment to be with his wife, Margaret, who was heavily pregnant. The birth of a son would have further enhanced his position within the royal family, but the child was a girl and named Joan, after her grandmother, Joan of Acre. She was born in early January and the cermony of churching, or purification, of Margaret Gavaston took place at the Friary in York on February 20th 1312. The King's favourite musician, 'King' Robert, and his minstrels provided entertainment at the celebration, receiving a handsome payment of 40 marks.[5] The birth of a child confirmed Gavaston's position as an 'adopted' member of the royal family, since his daughter was the great-granddaughter of Edward I. Gavaston planned to send his daughter to be educated at the convent at Amesbury, where the King's sister, Mary, resided, and he arranged for her to marry Thomas Wake, son of one of the lords of the northern Marches, but she died in infancy. Perhaps Gavaston's essay into fatherhood inspired the King to do the same, since his first legitimate child was born ten months later.[6]

Edward had already regained control of the Chancery by transferring it to York and he next attempted to take over the Exchequer. In effect, during the early months of 1312, there were two rival centres of government, as the King and Household remained in the north, while the Ordainers stayed in the south. In order to extend his influence further, Edward began to enlist men of proven ability to serve him personally. In spite of his earlier animosity to Walter Langton, who had been chief adviser to Edward I, the King restored his bishopric of Lichfield and Coventry and then appointed him Treasurer of the Exchequer 'until (the next) Parliament'.[7] The words 'until Parliament', were deliberately chosen to deflect criticism by the Ordainers, who wished to control such appointments. Clearly, Edward felt a temporary appointment might be more acceptable to them than a permanent one. However, the Exchequer office was still in London and the Ordainers ignored the new appointment. As a result, Edward was forced to yield and Walter of Norwich continued in office as Treasurer of the Exchequer.[8]

The King was more successful in other ways and organized a commission to negotiate with the Ordainers to review Ordinances which were considered to be harmful to him. Some of his supporters were also reinstated; for example, Isabella de Vescy regained Bamburgh Castle, while her brother, Henry Beaumont, again took control of the Isle of Man, and Gavaston took over Scarborough Castle, with orders to hand it over to no-one but the King.[9] At the same time, there were rumours that Edward had being trying to protect Gavaston from his enemies in both France and England by sending him to Scotland and that he had offered to give up claims to the overlordship of Scotland, if Gavaston could be safe there.[10]

The Ordainers, for their part, saw Gavaston's return as a threat to the country. Principally, they associated the enrichment of Gavaston with an empty Treasury when they saw the country's revenues flowing into the pocket of the royal favourite. In the event, Archbishop Winchelsey excommunicated Gavaston once more, on the grounds that his return and restoration were a threat to law and order. Chroniclers took the same view and were generally hostile to Gavaston; for example, the compiler of the *Annals of London* used the emotive word *seductor* (deceiver, seducer, traitor) to describe him at this time.[11] Although the leading nobles were understandably reluctant to take up arms against their King, the Earls of Arundel, Gloucester, Hereford, Lancaster, Pembroke, Surrey and Warwick were all united in an alliance to protect the Ordinances. They formed a plan in which Gloucester was responsible for the safety of London and the south of England; Hereford and Essex took control of the counties in the east, while Lancaster safeguarded the western counties and north Wales. Their supporters, Henry Percy and Robert Clifford, had the task of preventing the King and Gavaston from escaping into Scotland. In addition, Pembroke and Surrey intended to approach the King and capture Gavaston. Such measures were to be carried out on the pretext of holding tournaments, which gave an excuse for large gatherings of armed men. Thomas, Earl of Lancaster, now took the lead in the opposition to the King.[12] Lancaster had become the wealthiest and most influential opponent of Gavaston; he was the son of Edmund of Lancaster (a younger brother of Edward I) and Blanche, Queen of Navarre. His family connections meant that he was both the King's cousin and the Queen's uncle. Furthermore, he had acquired extensive estates by his marriage to the daughter of the Earl of Lincoln.

In anticipation of trouble, the King and Gavaston took refuge in Newcastle for a while, perhaps to give the Gascon time to recover from illness. Certainly, the King's Wardrobe accounts recorded payments to a doctor for looking after him there.[13] However, on May 4th 1312, Lancaster took the initiative by launching an attack on the city of Newcastle and took the royal party by surprise. The citizens made no attempt to protect the King and the city and castle were quickly taken. Edward and Gavaston escaped by boat from Tynemouth, abandoning the royal treasure, servants, weapons and horses. Isabella, who was pregnant, also fled and sought safety in York, leaving some of her possessions behind at South Shields in her haste to get away. While she accompanied her husband on his travels in the north, she wrote to her father, revealing how much she resented Gavaston for monopolizing her husband's attention.[14] In the meantime, Gavaston reached the safety of Scarborough Castle, which was already equipped with supplies to withstand a siege, while Edward returned to York.[15]

During the attack on Newcastle, the Earl of Lancaster had captured the King's treasure and his arms and equipment, while Pembroke and Surrey played their part in the plan and laid siege to Scarborough Castle. Within two weeks, supplies inside the castle had run short and, with hardly any supporters left, Gavaston was forced to surrender and ask for terms. It is difficult to know the truth of what happened; some writers have suggested that the King bribed Pembroke to treat Gavaston leniently, while others put forward the opinion that Gavaston himself influenced Pembroke to accept his surrender on favourable terms. Certainly, there is evidence that the King and Gavaston were able to remain in communication during the siege, perhaps with the aid of Pembroke.[16] In the event, Gavaston's men were allowed to remain at Scarborough, with the possibility that he might return there later. Clearly, some kind of an agreement was worked out which gave Edward hope of saving Gavaston. Pembroke had arranged to take his prisoner to Wallingford, to the Gascon's own castle, which had been restored to him earlier in the same year. But when the party reached Deddington (about 27 miles from Wallingford) Gavaston asked for a rest and so they stayed at the house of the rector there. Since Pembroke's wife was at Bampton, at a distance of about 20 miles from Deddington, the Earl went to visit her, leaving Gavaston unguarded.

The news that Gavaston was near soon reached Guy Beauchamp, Earl of Warwick, who collected a small force and approached the rectory. Chroniclers recorded the sequence of events, describing how Warwick, with about 140 men, drew near to Deddington on June 10th. At sunrise, the party reached the house where the Gascon was staying and surrounded it. When Gavaston realised his predicament and saw that there was no hope of escape this time, he surrendered to Warwick. The chroniclers saw Warwick as a hero, punishing this traitor who had betrayed and robbed the kingdom and they recorded Gavaston's reaction to Warwick, 'But when Peter saw him, he laughed and hurled insults from the window, calling him the Black Dog of Arden'.[17] In contrast to his showy costumes of earlier times, the Gascon wore just a simple tunic and his head and feet were bare. Warwick took him prisoner and transferred him to Warwick Castle, where he was kept under close arrest. Meanwhile, Gavaston's opponents gathered at Warwick to decide his fate. The Earl of Warwick handed over Gavaston to them, they gave him a form of trial in which they declared he was an enemy to the King, kingdom and people and sentenced him to be executed as a traitor.[18] The Earls removed him from Warwick's lands and, when they had reached Blacklow Hill, not far from Kenilworth, which lay within the lands of the Earl of Lancaster, they ordered his execution. Because he had married the daughter of the Earl of Gloucester and was therefore a nobleman by marriage, he was beheaded and was spared the hideous death of being disembowelled, which was the usual punishment for a traitor. Immediately after the execution, his opponents left and his body was carried by four shoemakers to Warwick for burial, but the Earl of Warwick, who had stayed within his castle during the execution, sent it back to Blacklow Hill. Finally, it was taken to the house of the Dominican Friars at Oxford, where it was kept under guard. Because Gavaston had been excommunicated, the friars did not dare to bury his body in consecrated ground.[19]

The execution was received in different ways. Some contemporaries recorded a great feeling of hatred against those who were responsible, referring to the atrocity of their action because they had executed a great nobleman, a man who was the King's adopted brother, his friend and close companion. However, others recorded how the country rejoiced in the fall of Gavaston, a man who was mourned only by his close friends and people who had prospered from his friendship.[20] Political songs, parodies of church songs, celebrated his death, 'The death of Peter has finally come; he reigned far too long. The evil tree is felled when Peter is beheaded'. Another song emphasised his pride and his wealth, 'The land, sea, stars, and all mankind rejoice in his fall. Ferocious and cruel above all, now his splendour has vanished'.[21]

The King, above all, mourned for his friend and cared for him even after death. While Gavaston's body lay unburied, the King and Margaret Gavaston paid for men to watch over it and for waxed cloths and a coffin.[22] Finally, the King obtained absolution from the excommunication order from the Pope and the elaborate funeral took place in January 1315, two and a half years after the execution. A special carriage, with five horses, took the body from Oxford to Langley, stopping at St Albans on the way. Three pavilions were transported from London and a huge amount of money was spent on the ceremony, which was was attended by a great number of dignitaries. Among those present were the King, the Archbishop, the Chancellor and Treasurer, together with the Earls of Pembroke and Hereford, Hugh Despenser the younger and Henry Beaumont. The Dominicans at Langley received a substantial annual grant from the Treasury:

> The Lord King, because of his affection for Peter de Gavastone, whom he called his brother, established a convent of Black Friars at Langley, where he was buried.[23]

The King also made generous provision for Gavaston's wife and daughter and his servants. A chronicler recalled the homosexual nature of their friendship and compared Edward's grief with the despair that overwhelmed King David on the death of his friend Jonathan, which showed 'a love which is reckoned to have gone beyond the love of women'. The King's generosity extended to former members of Gavaston's household and family. For example, when John Russell, who had been a groom in Gavaston's service, handed over to the King a horse which he claimed had belonged to his former master, he was rewarded with a sum of money. Gavaston's brother also had his debts paid by the King.[24]

On the face of it, the removal of Gavaston was a victory for the Ordainers since they had succeeded in destroying the one person whom they considered to be a threat to the safety of the country. However, the problems did not end with his death and their so-called victory had a divisive effect, one of which was the immediate transfer of the loyalties of the Earls of Pembroke and Surrey who, 'full of rage and anger', joined the King as he moved first to London and then to Canterbury. Despenser the younger, described by a chronicler as 'even worse than Gavaston', also supported the King. Others, who had been members of Gavaston's household rallied to the King and demanded revenge. The threat of civil war loomed yet again as 'continual hatred grew between the King and the Earls'.[25] Edward reacted quickly and sent out orders for castles and towns to be made secure and strong. He himself travelled to Dover, fortified the castle and secured the support of the Cinque Ports. On his return to London, he forbade anyone to come armed to Parliament and ordered 'certain Ordinances prejudicial to the Crown to be corrected'.[26]

In August 1312 the King made known his fury at the killing and sent messengers to the King of France, to the Pope, to various Cardinals and other church officials to explain the situation in England. The Pope responded by sending envoys to England to negotiate between the King and his nobles. He sent Cardinal Arnaud Novelli, formerly Abbot of Fontfroide in southern France, and another Arnaud, who became Cardinal-Bishop of Albano (Italy); these men were later joined by Louis, Count of Evreux, the brother of the King of France. Incidentally, the King took advantage of Novelli's presence in England and asked him to preside at the baptism of his first-born son in November 1312.

XIII   THE KING'S JEWELS

In the meantime, negotiations between the King's supporters and the nobles continued, as they tried to organize the surrender of the King's jewels and horses that had been captured at Newcastle. Problems had arisen because it was difficult to establish ownership of the property. Edward and Gavaston had escaped from Newcastle in a hurry, leaving considerable amounts of property behind, and it is very likely that the belongings of the two men became muddled. At the time of the attack, Lancaster had confiscated all the items and an inventory was made. If some of the jewels could be identified as Gavaston's, it would have been right and proper for them to have been granted to the King, as the confiscated property of a traitor. However, if the King accepted them on this basis, he was acknowledging Gavaston's treachery and justifying his execution. Such a decision would also affect the status of Gavaston's widow and daughter, who could not inherit the property of a traitor. It has been suggested that the jewels were, in fact, part of the royal treasure, which were held by Gavaston in his capacity as the King's Chamberlain and he may have been carrying them to provide emergency funds for the royal party.[1] To help resolve the problem, the Pope's envoys were installed at St Albans Abbey and the nobles were offered guarantees of safe conduct to allow them to meet the mediators at Markyate, about 15 miles from St Albans. However, the English nobles refused all their efforts at negotiation, on the grounds that these men were foreigners who could not understand their problems and they preferred to take the advice of their own English Bishops.[2] When Gilbert of Clare, Earl of Gloucester, eventually came forward to act as a mediator, the resolve of the other nobles weakened and a 'first treaty' *(Prima Tractatio)* was finally agreed in December 1312, as a basis for further negotiations.[3]

The first treaty should have given the Ordainers more or less what they had hoped for. For their part, they promised to grant the King's request for money if they were pardoned for their participation in the murder of Gavaston. They also asked for property that had been confiscated by the King or his officers to be restored to them and pleaded for their supporters, who had been unjustly imprisoned, to be set free. In return for these concessions, they offered to pay for 400 men-at-arms when

Edward next decided to invade Scotland and to return the captured jewels. However, as part of the treaty, they insisted that the Ordinances should be kept and that all those whom they regarded as 'evil counsellors' should be banished from contact with the King.[4] Two French lawyers, who were acting on behalf of the King, opposed the demands of the Ordainers saying that these men had not been elected and had no right to enforce such conditions.[5] The lawyers argued that the Ordinances were too vague and that they were contrary to the rights of the King, to *Magna Carta* and to the King's oath at the Coronation. They claimed that the Ordainers had made themselves excommunicate by opposing *Magna Carta*, and so had no legal power.

The Ordainers replied that they were not subject to written laws, but to traditional laws and customs and, if these were no longer valid, they should be changed by common consent. In this way, they were implying that the Ordinances were lawful, because they were based on consent. There was no real outcome to the dispute since the two sides were so far apart. Nevertheless, Edward recovered the jewels but no further decisions were made and negotiations dragged on. During this time there were also problems in the city of London.[6] On September 20th, when the King's officers, including the Earl of Pembroke, Despenser the younger, and John Cromwell, keeper of the Tower of London, went to the city to ask the citizens to support their King, there were riots around the Guildhall and the officials were forced to flee with their lives in danger. The following night, as a further symbol of protest, the local people tore down various protective structures that had been built around the Tower.[7]

XIV   A MEASURE OF AGREEMENT

While the negotiations with the Ordainers dragged on, Edward was at Windsor, where his son, later to be Edward III, was born on November 12th 1312. The King and Queen had been married for five years and Isabella was seventeen years old at the time. In spite of French requests that the baby should be named Louis after his French relations, he was called Edward after his father and grandfather and was baptized in the chapel of St Edward, within the castle. A few days after he was born. his father granted him the counties of Chester and Flint and he was given the title of Earl of Chester.[1] In a typically generous gesture, the King rewarded John Launge, a gentleman of Isabella's household, who brought him the news of the birth, and his wife, Joan, who attended the Queen, with the sum of £80 a year for life.[2] In contrast to the earlier unrest in London, the birth of the new Prince brought great rejoicing. The *Annals of London* recorded how the Mayor and aldermen led the dancing in the streets and the guilds and companies celebrated 'day and night'. The royal party spent Christmas at Windsor and, when the King and Queen returned to Westminster after Christmas, the Fishmongers' company welcomed them with a grand pageant. The members of the company, wearing clothes decorated with gold and showing the arms of England and France, rode to Westminster, taking with them a large model of a ship, complete with mast and sails, again bearing the arms of England and France. They further accompanied the Queen when she moved to Eltham in Kent, a journey of about seven miles. She stayed at the country house, later known as Eltham Palace, that Antony Bek, Bishop of Durham, had largely rebuilt and bequeathed to the King, who granted it to Isabella.[3]

The following year Edward and Isabella sailed to France, to attend the Coronation of Louis, the eldest son of Philip IV, as King of Navarre. They left Dover in the spring of 1313, travelling with a company of about 220 people, and first visited Aquitaine and then spent almost two months in Paris, where they enjoyed the entertainments provided by the French court. The King of France escorted them as far as Pontoise on their return journey but before they left for England, a fire broke out in their apartments during the night, Edward and Isabella escaped with their lives but lost many of their possessions.[4]

The visit had important financial results. The English lands in Gascony were expected to make a sizeable contribution to the Exchequer. However, the Ordinances of 1311 had criticized the administration of Gascony, declaring that, like Ireland and Scotland, it was a drain on the Exchequer rather than an advantage to it. New ministers were appointed, but there had been no noticeable improvement in revenues until negotiations between the King's officials and Pope Clement V provided a temporary remedy. The Pope was a Gascon and, seizing a chance to enrich his own family, he agreed to give Edward II a large loan, provided that the income from Gascony was handed over to him or to his nominees. After prolonged negotiations, the contract was eventually confirmed on October 28th 1313.[5] However, Edward himself received very little direct benefit from the loan, since the whole amount was handed over to the Italian financier, Antony of Pessagno, who then paid out sums of money for the upkeep of the Household and various royal necessities, while recouping his own expenses.[6]

Edward's foreign visit seemed a particularly reckless and ill-considered action when the Scots, led by Robert Bruce, were inflicting severe losses on the towns of Scotland and northern England. However, after the removal of Gavaston, relations between England and France had improved and Edward may have felt that friendship with the French King would be more useful to him than another campaign in Scotland. For the duration of his absence, he made his nephew, Gilbert of Clare, his regent and promised to make a settlement with the Ordainers when he returned from France.[7] However, Edward failed to return in time to meet them on July 8th, as he had agreed. He landed at Sandwich and made a leisurely journey through Kent, reaching London in August, when the nobles had grown tired of waiting and left. As a result, it was September before the two sides met and an agreement was finally reached. This time the King took the initiative and invited the nobles to a meeting at which he kissed each one and granted them pardon for the murder of Gavaston. In return, they knelt to him and acknowledged him as their sovereign. So, by prolonging and postponing the negotiations, Edward had cleverly managed to make peace while still refusing to recognise the Ordinances. The removal of Gavaston finally brought reconciliation and the occasion was celebrated with a magnificent banquet in October 1313. We may discern the influence of Isabella in bringing about this settlement. 'The Queen anxiously interceded, striving to calm the feelings of both parties and strenuously attempting to make peace'. The document of pardon stated that 'this pardon and remission is granted by the King, through the prayers of his dearest companion, Isabella, Queen of England'.[8]

The King also gained further support by securing the appointment of his Chancellor, Walter Reynolds, as Archbishop of Canterbury. Following the death of Archbishop Winchelsey in 1313, the monks at Canterbury claimed the right to choose his successor and they appointed Thomas Cobham. However, Edward persuaded Clement V to overrule this decision and, amid allegations of simony (an exchange of money in return for church office), Reynolds was appointed on October 1st 1313.[9] Winchelsey had been a strong-minded and independent man, who had been at the forefront of political life. He felt he had taken on the role of his distant predecessor, Thomas Becket, in his opposition to the King. He had provided strong leadership to the other Ordainers and his death was a serious loss to them. In contrast to Winchelsey, Reynolds was a supporter of Gavaston; the two men had been in Edward's Household when he was Prince of Wales, Reynolds had lent his house in London to the Gascon and he had been involved in conducting secret business with the Pope concerning his return to England.[10] The author of the *Life of Edward II* was bitterly hostile to the appointment of Reynolds, ascribing his influence to his skills at organizing theatrical shows *(ludi theatricales)* which delighted and entertained the King.[11]

Describing this stage in the King's reign, the same writer made scathing comments, suggesting that, after being on the throne for six years, his only achievement was to produce a son to ensure the succession. The author contrasts the very unheroic character of Edward II to the bravery of Richard I. Clearly, contemporaries found it difficult to understand Edward's apparent lack of interest in being King.[12] His disdain for politics contrasted strongly to his other interests. For example, on the eve of Palm Sunday in 1314 he visited St Albans Abbey and made an offering of a gold cross decorated with precious gems, which contained relics of the saint. At the same time, he entrusted himself and his companions to the protection of the saint. When he discovered that his father had intended to renew the buildings of the choir, he was fired with his usual enthusiasm for buildings and he offered to provide 100 marks in cash and timber from Dinsley, a former Templar estate in Hertfordshire. He ordered that no expense should be spared since it was for the honour of God and St Alban, the first English martyr. Traditionally, it was believed that Alban was executed at the Roman town of Verulamium in the early fourth century, during the persecution of the Christians ordered by the Emperor Diocletian. According to Bede, a church had been built on the site, which was later superseded by the abbey church of St Alban. There was also a story that the body of St Alban had been taken to Ely for safety at the time of Danish attacks and that the monks at Ely refused to restore it when the danger was past. However, the monks of St Albans always claimed that they had sent away a duplicate body and had kept the original.

The day after Palm Sunday, the King went to Ely Cathedral, where he celebrated Easter. While he was there, the monks told him that they had the body of St Alban at Ely. The King immediately asked to see what was in the tomb which was ascribed to St Alban. He said to the Bishop of Ely, 'You know that the brothers at St Albans think they truly have the body of the saint, while the monks in this place claim to have the same body. I wish to find out where I should pay my respects to the relics of the saint'. When the monks heard this 'they went pale', not knowing what to say. They were afraid of losing their treasure if it really was St Alban, but they would be accused of deceit, if it was not the body of the saint. No-one really knew what lay inside the tomb. The King watched the nails of the coffin being removed and even went forward to lift the lid for himself. When the watchers looked in, they were surprised to see that the coffin was completely filled with a rough cloth, part of which was spattered with fresh blood. They decided that this must be the vestment of St Alban–the one that he wore when he was martyred and the blood had been preserved by a miracle. For the first time, the monks knew what relic they had and the King was happy to discover the truth. He gave the monks many gifts and stayed there for a while, delighted that St Alban could now be truly venerated in two special places. The chronicler knowingly remarked that the tomb was opened by a monk named Alan, who afterwards held the office of Prior 'because of his useful services'.[13]

During this time, Isabella was in France. In March 1314 she had gone to Paris with the Earl of Gloucester to negotiate with Louis X, the new King of France, who had succeeded his father, Philip, in 1313. Because of this change, it was necessary to confirm earlier agreements made about Gascony with the new King. In May, the Queen's party was joined by the Earl of Pembroke and, as a result of various negotiations, Louis agreed to uphold the arrangements formerly made by his father. Edward was satisfied with the outcome and concentrated his attention on Scotland.[14]

XV   BANNOCKBURN

Although the Ordainers no longer had Gavaston as a focus for their hostility, there was no obvious improvement in the King's attitude and he was still quite unwilling to accept any reforms or any kind of restraint on his actions. However, the affairs of Scotland once more began to influence English politics. While the negotiations had been going on between the King and the Ordainers, Bruce had taken advantage of their preoccupation both to consolidate his power base in Scotland and to launch attacks on the English. His forces were strong enough to besiege the town of Perth, which was then in English hands, and capture it. After the fall of Perth, other Scottish towns and strongholds also came under his control. Following these successes, he then marched into England, reaching as far south as Chester. He also recaptured the Isle of Man, which was an important base for ships moving along the west coast. The Scots were particularly well-equipped for these marauding raids; they did not travel with heavy armour and the encumbrances of large baggage-trains like the English. On the contrary, their forces were lightly armed and highly manoeuvrable, carrying all their equipment with them. Bruce now controlled large areas of Scotland and, apart from castles on the Border, only Stirling remained as the main English base in Scotland. On the orders of Sir Thomas Rokeby, the castle had been strongly fortified and well-supplied. He had ensured that it was equipped with strong defences and platforms for launching artillery attacks and it was manned with light-horsemen, men-at-arms, watchmen and archers. Carpenters and stonemasons had prepared the defences, surrounding the armaments with timber walls that had been covered with clay and turf to protect them against fire. Two springs had been diverted to provide a secure water-supply.[1]

The Border fortresses of Berwick, Dunbar, Linlithgow and Roxburgh, were able to hold out against the Scots for a while, principally because the Borderers did not generally support Bruce. But in the autumn of 1313 the people of the Borders sent a desperate petition to the King, declaring that, since his departure three years previously, they had suffered continual losses. They had been forced to hand over their corn to the Scots and their livestock was stolen, partly by the Scots and partly by the English garrisons at Berwick and Roxburgh. They had given money to Bruce to call off his men, but then men from the garrison at Berwick came and took the people from their beds, 'carrying them off, dead and alive, and holding them to ransom'. The King thanked them for their petition and made a formal commitment to lead an army to Scotland the following year.[2] During 1313 the Scots were besieging Stirling Castle, but without success. The result was a stalemate, since they were unable to capture it, nor was there any hope of relief for the English garrison trapped inside. In this situation, Bruce made a pact with the constable, Sir Philip Mowbray, that if no help arrived before Midsummer day (June 24th) 1314, the English would surrender. Clearly, Bruce did not anticipate that Edward would mount another campaign.[3] Disparaging comments by the chroniclers emphasised the King's idleness and failure to act, but he had already been planning a further campaign in Scotland and this new challenge spurred him on. He left behind the monks of Ely and moved on to Lincoln, then York and Newcastle, eventually arriving at Berwick.

Even with such a threat from the north, the English lords failed to unite against the Scots. The Earl of Lancaster adamantly refused to join the campaign because the summons had not come from Parliament, as required by the Ordinances, while Arundel, Surrey and Warwick were similarly unwilling to follow the King. There were others, however, who were not so stubborn, and the Earls of Gloucester, Hereford and Pembroke served with the King. It is difficult to estimate the size of his army; various sources suggest any number between 20,000 and 200,000, but it was certainly a large force, with a preponderance of cavalry. Clearly, the English had learned from previous campaigns that cavalry was important for manoeuvrability over such uneven ground. A vast supply-train of baggage and provision waggons followed the main force. A chronicler suggested that the sheer size of the English army caused the King to be over-confident. 'He hurried on day by day to the pre-arranged place, as if he was going to St James's, not leading an army to war'. There was also criticism that the halts for rest and food were far too brief, with the result that the soldiers were exhausted by the speed of travel. Others, writing with hindsight, stressed the King's incompetence in advancing without adequate planning and allowing his troops to ravage and plunder in England, as if they were in an enemy country.[4]

In fact, some of the criticism was unjustified since the King had begun his planning well in advance. For example, he had cancelled the summons to a meeting of Parliament scheduled for Westminster at Easter, since he was intending to set out for Newcastle, and he asked Lancaster and others to meet him in the north, ready for war. He also wrote to the Archbishop of Canterbury, ordering him to enforce the collection of taxes from the clergy to provide money for the campaign.[5] In preparation for war, he had issued orders for equipment, sending Adam, his fletcher, from Selbourne, in Hampshire, to the Forest of Dean, in Gloucestershire, to collect arrow shafts and quivers and transport them to Newcastle. Similarly, there were orders for bows and bowstrings and for 'a great hammer and an iron crowbar' to break up and lift stones. Such heavy siege-engines, crossbows and crossbow bolts were an important part of the equipment and five great siege-engines were transported from Berwick to Roxburgh along the River Tweed. There were also orders for armour, tents and transport waggons. During Edward's previous campaigns in Scotland, there had been supply problems because of the lack of mills north of the Border and, to overcome this difficulty, he ordered a windmill to be set up at Edinburgh, which would grind the corn to feed his forces. Just as in previous campaigns, the east coast ports provided ships and sailors to convey food and materials to Newcastle and Berwick. Edward had also commanded 30 'of the best ships' from the south coast ports between Shoreham and Plymouth to assemble at Winchelsea and then sail to Skinburness, on the Solway Firth, to protect the western seas. However, most of them refused to sail; the men of Winchelsea declared that they had supplied two ships, but that the weather prevented them from setting out. While preparing for war, the King took recreation in the form of hunting and gambling. He probably also spent time listening to music, since there were payments to bagpipers and fiddlers, as well as to a trumpeter and other musicians.[6]

The English forces assembled first at Berwick, where the Household was based. By June 21st they had reached Edinburgh from where they set out towards Stirling. At this juncture, Bruce moved from his position near Falkirk towards Stirling, hoping to prevent the English from raising the siege. Since there are no contemporary accounts of the battle, we do not know the exact site where the two armies met. However, we know that Bruce took his stand about two miles from Stirling Castle near a small stream, known as the Bannock, which flowed into the River Forth. On the evening before Midsummer day, which was the last day agreed for the relief of Stirling, the English army came into sight and a few minor skirmishes took place. Bruce himself fought in fierce single combat against Humphrey Bohun, Earl of Hereford, and finally struck him down with a battleaxe. The next morning the whole English army approached the Scottish forces. The cavalrymen charged but they were trapped in the marshy ground around the stream. They could not make any headway against the array of Scottish pikemen and, while they were in such a state of confusion, the Scots rushed among them and slaughtered them. The English infantry hardly entered the battle and the archers could not be fully deployed without endangering their own men. The King himself was not in immediate danger, but his nephew, Gilbert of Clare, Earl of Gloucester, who led the cavalry charge, was killed. Gloucester was then aged 23 and a poet described him standing gloriously in the thick of battle, like a hero of ancient Greece.[7]

After the first stage of the battle, Bruce ordered his non-combatants to line the hilltop behind his army, giving the impression that a second army was about to join the fray. When the English soldiers saw this second 'army' coming, they began to waver. As Bruce led his charge on the main body of the English troops, the men turned and ran, and many were drowned in the river. The King himself was no coward and he refused to join the fleeing army until the Earl of Pembroke seized his horse's reins, forcing him to leave the field. They rode past Stirling, which was now surrendered to the Scots, and reached the comparative safety of Dunbar. All the English baggage was left lying on the field of battle for the Scots to plunder. The great siege-engines were also abandoned. The battle of Bannockburn resounded as a victory for the Scots. They took many English prisoners, keeping the knights for ransom or exchange and killing others. Edward's first full-scale military campaign as King had proved to be a disaster. The chroniclers unreservedly blamed him and his lack of leadership for the defeat. The *Chronicle of Lanercost*, compiled at Lanercost Priory in Cumberland, which suffered heavily from incursions by the Scots, contrasted the successes of Edward I to the disasters of his son. The chronicler took a moral stance saying that, when Edward I went on a campaign against the Scots, he visited the shrines of the English saints, going to Canterbury, Bury St Edmunds, Lincoln and Durham, where he made offerings and distributed gifts to monasteries and to the poor. Edward II did none of this, but 'marching with great pomp and elaborate state, he took goods from the monasteries on his journey and, as was reported, did things to the prejudice and injury of the saints'. To the monks of Lanercost, Bannockburn was 'an evil, miserable and calamitous day'.[8]

Most of the criticism of Edward II is derived from chronicles which were written with hindsight, generally after his death. However, there are just a few indications of contemporary opinion which confirm the views of the chroniclers. For example, in July 1314, soon after the disaster at Bannockburn, Robert le Messager, who was a member of the Household, declared that nobody could expect Edward to win battles when he spent his time in idleness and 'in making ditches and digging and in other improper occupations', instead of hearing the Mass. Le Messager was charged with speaking disrespectfully about the King and was put in prison for his offence, but was released at the request of Isabella. There was another case at Oxford, where a man was charged with insulting the King;

he, too, was later released, which suggests that their opinions were not a surprise to their contemporaries.[9]

While Bannockburn brought criticism of the King into the open, the death of the Earl of Gloucester at the age of 23 was a severe blow to Edward. He had been one of the most influential nobles and had acted as regent when the King was in France in 1312. He had remained on good terms with Edward and his moderate views and negotiating skills had helped to smooth out various differences between the King and the Ordainers. He held extensive estates in East Anglia, Kent and Surrey, south-west England, south Wales and Ireland, but he had no heir. Edward allowed his widow, Maud, to maintain that she was pregnant for about two years, probably because the birth of an heir would prevent the breakup of such vast estates; also the King would have the benefit of wardship of the lands until an heir came of age. However, no child was born and, as a result, the large inheritance was divided between Gloucester's three sisters, Margaret, widow of Piers Gavaston, who later married Hugh Audley, Eleanor, wife of Hugh Despenser the younger, and Elizabeth, who first married Theobald Verdon, then John Burgh, and finally Roger Damory. Disputes about the division of this inheritance were to cause many problems during the later years of Edward's reign.[10]

XVI   AFTER BANNOCKBURN

Apart from the large death toll among the English soldiers, the immediate effect of Bannockburn was to make Robert Bruce a national hero. In the months that followed the battle, the Scots launched countless raids into northern England which continued throughout 1315. Robert's brother, Edward, also took advantage of the victory to extend the war into Ireland.

The defeat, and the loss of so many of his supporters, drove Edward II to rely on the Ordainers, men whom he had earlier regarded as his enemies. A meeting of Parliament was called at York in September 1314, in the aftermath of Bannockburn, but the King did not attend; he stayed at Wolston, in Warwickshire, and wrote on September 7th authorizing the Bishop of Exeter, the Earl of Pembroke and Henry Beaumont to open the session in his place. However, the inclusion of Beaumont caused some consternation among the Ordainers and further letters were sent the same day, omitting Beaumont's name and substituting that of the Bishop of Worcester, who was more acceptable to the Ordainers.[1] At the meeting, the Ordainers firmly attributed Edward's defeat to his stubborn refusal to uphold the Ordinances and, since they were now in a strong enough position to impose their wishes on the King, they ensured that their own supporters became his advisers. Above all, Edward was forced to rely on the Earl of Lancaster, who had refused to join the Scottish campaign because it had not been agreed in Parliament. Lancaster, instead of opposing the King, now became one of his principal advisers. The death of Gavaston had removed the chief reason for opposition and the nobles now tried to work with the King, rather than against him. They began by re-organizing the Household and aimed to make changes that were far more wide-ranging than those proposed in 1311 when the Ordinances were first issued. The Ordainers appointed John Sandale as Chancellor and confirmed the appointment of Walter of Norwich as Treasurer. They went even further and replaced most of the county sheriffs, on the grounds that the former officers were the King's men. Since the office of sheriff included military as well as administrative duties, we can see that the Ordainers were demanding, and taking, extensive powers.[2] Edward was also forced to promise that there would be a perambulation of the forests (an official survey to record the boundaries in order to establish rights of possession). The policy of removing men whom the Ordainers identified as hostile to the Ordinances and of having undue influence over the King was continued at meetings of Parliament during the early months of 1315, when Beaumont, Despenser the younger and others were forced to leave the court. While these measures had political repercussions, they were also aimed at reducing the costs of the Household and a chronicler claimed that there was a saving of £10 a day in costs.[3]

Furthermore, the Ordainers attempted to organize the restoration of lands that had been taken by the King. They set a date of March 1310 and declared that any lands granted by the King since that date should be restored to their former owners. While this might seem to be a reasonable proposition, the practical difficulties were immense and it angered those who had received legitimate grants from the King after that date; for example, Beaumont was forced to give up the Isle of Man, which had been recovered from Scottish control, and the Earl of Surrey had to surrender the castle and estates of High Peak in Derbyshire, formerly held by Gavaston. However, as a symbol of the new-found political unity, the King held a great banquet at Westminster in April 1315, attended by the Archbishop of Canterbury and the nobles. Ironically, this symbolic celebration of reconciliation was followed by a fire which damaged the great hall.[4] In theory, the changes proposed by the Ordainers should have resulted in the Ordinances being observed and improvements in the royal finances. However, other factors came into play and the years 1314-1316 proved to be highly disastrous and extremely disorderly. It was a period of floods, famine and private wars. Extreme weather conditions and shortages of food throughout the country caused economic upheaval as prices rose to excessively high levels. The problems were not restricted to the British Isles; famine swept across the whole of Europe. There had been so much rain in 1314 that it was difficult to collect in the harvest and Parliament was forced to issue Ordinances regulating the prices of foodstuffs. These attempted to fix the price and quality of items such as cattle, pigs, sheep, geese, chickens, pigeons and eggs but the shortages were so great that price regulations were not effective and the legislation was later repealed. The summer of 1315 was even worse and torrential rain lasted from the beginning of May until the autumn. Floods were widespread across the whole of Europe, the harvest failed once again and it was impossible to sow the crops for the following year. The crisis even had a direct effect on the royal family; when the King and the Household stopped at St Albans, there was hardly any bread to be found for them.[5]

However, in spite of these difficulties, there was no evidence of austerity when the King and Queen visited the port of Winchelsea in Sussex during the summer of 1315. New Winchelsea had been founded as a new town by Edward I in 1292 to replace the old one, which had been encroached upon by the sea. It was laid out in a regular grid pattern, to a design that was unusual in England, but already familiar in Caernarvon and other new towns in north Wales constructed during the reign of Edward I. The new harbour at Winchelsea had brought prosperity to the town and there was plenty of food and wine for the royal visitors. The Queen attended Mass and her chaplain, Master Thomas Buchard, offered gifts to the church on her behalf. The new town had a magnificent parish church, dedicated to St Thomas Becket. Among the decorations of the church, two finely-carved heads representing Edward and Isabella can be seen. After leaving the town, the King and Queen visited Hastings and both presented gifts to the chapel within the castle. Entertainment during the visit was provided by musicians. The King gave money to John the harpist, to Robert the fiddler, both of Hastings, and to Thomas the harpist of Winchelsea, for playing for him in the chapel at Hastings.[6] The prosperity of Winchelsea was based on trade with France and it is significant that the one area which did not suffer from the general shortages of food was Gascony, where there was a surplus of corn and wine in 1315.

During 1315 the Scottish raids into northern England forced the English to mount yet another campaign in the north and troops and transport were again summoned to the Borders. The Earl of Pembroke was put in charge of the area between the River Trent and Roxburgh, taking with him a large force, including 500 men-at-arms.[7] But large numbers like this were not effective against a smaller force with good local knowledge. The Scots continued their attacks and sacked Hartlepool, in County Durham, so thoroughly that the inhabitants had to abandon the town and escape by sea.[8] The Scots also besieged Carlisle, a city which blocked their raids on the western side of the country. If they had succeeded in taking it, most of northern England would have fallen under Scottish control.[9] But Carlisle was strongly fortified and the Scots abandoned the siege after ten days. They withdrew, devastating the surrounding countryside as they left. The English soldiers followed the retreating Scots, but they suffered heavy losses and many were taken prisoner.[10] At the same time, Edward Bruce, brother of Robert, was in Ireland, attempting to rouse the Irish people against the English. After successes in Ireland, Edward Bruce hoped to cross to Wales and incite the Welsh to rebel in a similar fashion.[11] However, Edward II sent orders to supply the castles of Dublin and Carrickfergus and the town of Dundalk, while the English fleet patrolled the Irish coast. In the event, Bruce's plan failed when Edmund Butler, Earl of Carrick, led an attack on the Scottish army in Ireland and defeated it.

Pembroke's lack of success in Scotland led to the appointment of Lancaster to take charge in the north, who had now became a military commander, as well as adviser to the King. Perhaps Lancaster's military appointment was one of desperation, since Pembroke and the local landowners had failed to achieve any victories, leaving Edward with virtually no alternative. In spite of problems in the north, the King spent time happily in Cambridgeshire and Huntingdonshire. He kept to his usual diversions and went to the fens and marshlands, taking with him a large crowd of country people, the kind of company he relished, with whom he was able to relax and enjoy himself and 'refresh his spirit'. He went rowing on the various stretches of water and, on one occasion, fell into the water and almost drowned. Then, leaving his companions and the pleasures of water-sports, he moved on to spend Christmas at Clipstone, near Nottingham, at the royal country house or hunting-lodge in Sherwood Forest to which Edward I had added elaborate new apartments and stables for 200 horses. The King's liking for music is a constant feature of the records and, in addition to his Welsh harpists and crowders he acquired a bagpiper, whom he sent abroad to improve his skills. After Christmas, the King went to Lincoln for a meeting of Parliament.[12]

Parliament was summoned for January 28th 1316 and it proved to be an extraordinary meeting. It had been called to deal with the critical state of affairs in Scotland, rebellion in Wales and other matters of importance, such as the failure of the economic regulations of 1314. However, the King and some of his advisers had already been holding discussions for two weeks before Lancaster and his supporters put in an appearance, with the result that there had to be 'a second opening of Parliament' on February 12th, when they eventually arrived. At this meeting, the ineffective legislation about price-controls was revoked, another campaign was planned for Scotland, headed by Lancaster and Thomas of Brotherton, the King's young half-brother, the King was granted the funds that he wanted (including a further tax on the clergy) and most participants went home.[13] But this was not the end of the assembly; on Sunday, February 22nd, there was a further meeting before the King in Lincoln Cathedral. On this occasion, Sir John Ros made a violent assault on Despenser the younger, attacking him verbally and then drawing his sword. Despenser retaliated by hitting Ros and wounding him. Finally, the two men were separated and placed under arrest.[14] Perhaps this quarrel was a symptom of the general discontent with appointments within the Household. Certainly, many of the King's officials had been replaced after Bannockburn, but Edward had gradually brought his own men back into official positions. To counter this move, the Ordainers planned further reforms of the Household.

It was decided that forces, led by the King and his nobles, would stay in the north during the coming winter, with the Earls paying their own expenses. The cost of keeping and supplying armies was enormous, especially during a time of famine when prices were so high. The combination of shortages of food and expensive military campaigns proved to be disastrous since lack of money meant that the army was hardly ever at full strength, which ensured that the campaigns were not a success. We can see the effects of natural disasters and shortages in the town of Berwick. The commanders sent desperate messages to the King, describing the suffering and losses within the town, where the men were starving and many were dead or wounded. One letter referred to conditions that were so bad that men preferred to risk death by going out to fight for food than to stay behind the walls and die of starvation. In February 1316 Maurice Berkeley, keeper of Berwick, had written to the royal officials:

> No town was ever in such distress. The garrison are deserting daily. Whenever a horse dies the men-at-arms carry off the flesh and boil and eat it. It is a pity to see Christians leading such a life.[15]

The situation was made worse because even when provisions were ordered for Berwick they did not arrive. In March the King sent Berkeley's plea to his Chancellor and Treasurer, ordering them to take action quickly to supply the garrison.[16] Eventually, provisions of wheat, wine and other items were dispatched by sea, intended for Berwick and Newcastle, but the ships were wrecked, or the contents stolen, before they reached their destination.[17]

Edward called for troops to muster at Newcastle in July 1316 but this was postponed until August 20th. There were repeated orders for taxation of the clergy and there was an order for money to be raised in Gascony but, after a further postponement, the campaign was eventually abandoned.[18] The two years that followed Bannockburn were highly successful for the Scots; Bruce had gained control over the whole of Scotland, he had besieged Berwick and Newcastle and raged so furiously through the Borders that the land was totally devasted. The economic hardships continued in England during 1316, when there were further outbreaks of disease, again followed by famine and high prices. Diseases also killed animals and caused further deaths among humans who ate the infected meat. In these circumstances, the terms set out in the Ordinances, which were meant to control the Kings' expenses, had very little effect. Parliament once more introduced laws in an attempt to keep prices low, dictating the level at which people might live and, in particular, limiting the number of courses to be served at mealtimes in wealthy households.[19] But,

Fourteenth-century painting in Westminster Abbey, believed to be of Edward II.

The Coronation of a King, possibly Edward II. The King is shown sitting on his Coronation chair attended by priests and courtiers. The faces of the people can be seen looking through a grille on the top left.

The Weeping King, believed to be Edward II, part of the tomb of John of Eltham in Westminster Abbey.

Castle Rising, Norfolk, Queen Isabella's final residence.

Berkeley Castle, Gloucestershire, the scene of Edward II's murder.

Edward II, King of England, and Isabella, daughter of Philip, King of France, depicted in a treatise by Walter de Milemete.

The execution of Hugh Despenser the younger at Hereford.

Effigy of Edward II in Gloucester Cathedral.

in reality, no amount of regulation could cope with such disasters. They affected the King directly since frequent occurrences of disease, famine, with the resultant shortages, reduced the value of his income. The incidence of disease among sheep reduced the revenues from wool, so that the estates of both the nobles and the King failed to produce the levels of income they had seen in earlier years. As incomes fell, so prices increased, and wheat cost 40 shillings a quarter, compared with a price of about 5 shillings a quarter in 1313. In addition, the money raised by taxation often failed to reach the Exchequer. Loans could provide short-term relief, but the combination of military campaigns in the north and country-wide famine caused huge problems. Shortages and hunger forced law-abiding people to resort to crime to obtain food and, as a result, the systems for maintaining law and order began to break down. Faced with this situation, the ambitions of the Ordainers to provide financial stability for the country were doomed to failure. Furthermore, a rebellion during the same year in south Wales threatened to develop into a general uprising throughout the Principality.

Llewellyn Bren, who had formerly been an official of Gilbert of Clare, Earl of Gloucester, resented his loss of authority after the Earl's death. He therefore decided to take advantage of the widespread unrest to protest against oppression by the royal agents who were then managing the Clare estates and he launched an attack against Caerphilly Castle in Glamorgan. This revolt, like the Scottish raids on northern England, brought a further drain on the Treasury, as more forces had to be enrolled against the attackers. In February 1316, the King ordered men from the Forest of Dean to take action against the Welsh insurgents whilst he himself raised troops throughout Wales to crush them. The Earl of Hereford led the English side, since his lands in Brecon bordered on Glamorgan; he was supported by Roger Mortimer of Chirk and his nephew, Roger Mortimer of Wigmore, William Montague and others, whose lands were threatened by the uprising. Eventually Bren was forced to surrender and was imprisoned. The King promised him a pardon, but he was executed at Cardiff on the order of Despenser the younger.[20]

The same year, the citizens of Bristol were defeated after a dispute that had been simmering for several years with the constable of the castle, Bartholomew Badlesmere. They had resented the imposition of new customs dues and the exemption of the more important citizens from payment. They also challenged the right of the King's Justices to pass judgement on matters that the citizens regarded as their business. On June 13th 1316, when Richard Ryvere, sheriff of the county of Gloucester, had arrested several outlaws in the city, the citizens retaliated by setting them free. As the sheriff returned and explained to the citizens assembled in the

Guildhall that he was ordered by the King to apprehend the outlaws, they refused to hand them over. He left but returned with an armed force to find the city fortified against him, 'and the whole community raised in war against the King, having associated with them a multitude of malefactors from Bayonne (France) and Wales'. They besieged the King's castle, drained the moat around it, destroyed the mill, constructed their own defences and brought in siege-engines, 'in express rebellion against the King, with banners raised'. Finally, to subdue the rebels, the King sent an armed force to Bristol and he ordered Maurice Berkeley, of nearby Berkeley Castle, to mount a guard along the estuary of the River Severn to cut off the city from the sea. The King's forces continued to defend the castle, where they mounted siege-engines and used them to break down the city walls. Eventually, on July 26th, the citizens were forced to surrender under the onslaught and the ringleaders were imprisoned.[21] Although this began as an internal dispute between two groups of citizens, it was used as an example of the King's incompetence, showing his failure to apply a firm hand *(manus rigida)*, which resulted in wicked men gaining power, while the innocent were punished. The King's court was seen as the source of such evil, where greedy men ruled supreme:

> Once, indeed, people were delighted to see the King's face when he came, but now, because the King's arrival brings trouble, they are very pleased when he leaves and, when he goes, they pray that he may never come back.[22]

Much of the criticism stemmed from the King's lack of money. In spite of continual requests for taxes upon the clergy and upon the people of Gascony, there was never enough money in the Treasury. Wherever he, or his court, or his armies went, they took supplies from the locality. Sometimes they paid market prices but, more often, they requisitioned supplies for royal use leaving a trail of devastation behind them. Furthermore, while the King was at York in August 1316, he sent out a demand that people holding land worth £50 or more should serve in the army without pay.[23] This independent action, taken without the consent of Parliament, totally contravened the Ordinances, 'which the King's officers broke whenever they had the chance'.[24] Certainly, the King's order was a direct challenge to the Ordainers, an act which predictably aroused the fury of the Earl of Lancaster. Lancaster's reaction was so fierce that the King felt obliged to arm himself against attack. Chroniclers again blamed the King's advisers for his thoughtless actions and described them as:

Men who stir up discord and many problems for the kingdom daily attending the Lord King, continually supporting his arrogance and lawless designs.[25]

There was further aggravation when the King, having gathered money and supplies for a Scottish campaign, was forced to abandon it, because the revenues were not sufficient for a full-scale campaign.

XVII NEW COURTIERS

While the King stayed at York, the Queen gave birth to another son, who was named John of Eltham. He was born in July 1316 at Eltham, near London, in the country house that had been granted to Isabella. The King was clearly pleased to hear of the birth of his second son and gave the messenger who brought the news a gift of £100. While still at York, he asked the Dominicans to pray for the royal family and especially for John of Eltham and, when he was at Lincoln, he made a grant of £500 to the Queen's nurse.[1] Isabella asked the Bishop of Norwich and the Earl of Lancaster to be sponsors for her son and the baptism took place at Eltham on August 30th:

> John of Fontenoy, clerk of the Queen's chapel, received one piece of Turkey cloth, and one of cloth of gold, for arraying the font in which the Lord John, son of the King, was baptized at Eltham. To Stephen Taloise, the Queen's tailor, were delivered five pieces of white velvet for making a robe against the churching of the Queen, after the birth of her son.[2]

As soon as the Queen had recovered from the birth, she set out to meet the King, arriving in York at the end of September. The election of a new Pope at Avignon in August 1316 brought a further change. Following the death of Pope Clement, Edward was hoping to enlist the help of his successor, John XXII, to solve some of his problems. He needed the Pope's support for his campaigns against Scotland, principally for financial reasons. Edward wanted to change the repayment terms for the loans made to him by Clement; he also wished to delay the fulfilment of his promise, made in 1313, to go on a crusade, and he hoped to enforce a further tax on the clergy, ostensibly to pay for the postponed crusade. The King sent Pembroke, with other envoys, to Avignon and they completed their task by April 1317. As a result of their pleas, Pope John allowed Edward to postpone the crusade; he provided the King with a five-year loan, raised from a tax on the clergy; and the repayment terms to Clement V were renegotiated. However, the new Pope intervened in an unexpected way. He appointed two Cardinals, Gaucelin d'Eauze and Luke Fieschi, to negotiate a peace settlement between England and Scotland.[3]

When the King abandoned his Scottish campaign of 1316, he left Edmund Fitzalan, Earl of Arundel, to protect the northern areas of England against the incursions of the Scots. Many pitiful cases show the extent of the devastation caused by the wars. For example, a certain Hugh Gray petitioned the King, declaring that he had served both the present King and his father in the Scottish wars, that he had been taken prisoner three times and, during the time of war, had lost all the income from his lands in Northumberland. His wife and children were captured at Berwick and he was forced to pay to ransom them and their possessions. He had nothing left, unless the King paid him his wages. Others, who had been wounded, were sent to monasteries, where they were cared for at the King's expense. But the monasteries had also suffered and there were many requests for help from religious establishments which had been burned and plundered and now had nothing.[4]

The King was severely criticized because he had failed to pursue the war against the Scots but, when we view this against the economic conditions of 1314-16, his actions become understandable. Although the country could not afford war, various chroniclers and the Ordainers firmly blamed the King's advisers for the lack of activity. The year 1317 followed the same trend as the two previous years in terms of economic difficulties and political problems, but the main difference lay in the influence of courtiers who were the successors to Gavaston. The chief targets for disapproval were the Despensers and three others, Roger Damory, Hugh Audley and William Montague, described by chroniclers as 'three hopefuls', who had risen in the shadow of the King's wings, men who were flattering favourites, even worse than Gavaston. These, like Gavaston, were regarded as men of no account, totally dependent on the King for wealth and position, whose influence over Edward was quite out of proportion to their rank and responsibilities. But the King trusted them and bound them to him by patronage. In effect, the death of Gavaston had brought no advantage to the country, since it allowed greedy men like this to flourish.[5]

Foremost among these were the two Despensers, elder and younger. Hugh Despenser the elder had served both Edward I and Edward II in wars in Wales, Flanders and Scotland and had been closely involved in diplomatic missions on their behalf, while the younger Despenser had been a member of the Household of Edward II when he was Prince of Wales and had been knighted with him in 1306. Edward II held him in high regard and rewarded him by granting him marriage with Eleanor of Clare, one of the sisters of the Earl of Gloucester. By virtue of marriage to Eleanor, the younger Despenser received the lordship of Glamorgan, in south Wales, which was the most important of the Clare holdings, together with estates in Devon, Somerset and Sussex. In the same way, Edward used marriage with a Clare heiress to reward his other friends, Roger Damory and Hugh Audley. By their marriages to these women, who were nieces of the King, the three men became members of the royal family and were placed at the forefront of the nobility. At the King's insistence, Damory married the reluctant Elizabeth of Clare, who had already been twice widowed. By his marriage, Damory acquired the Verdon estates in the Midlands, by virtue of his wife's previous marriage to Theobald Verdon, and the Clare estates in Norfolk and Suffolk, together with other manors, including the lordship of Usk in south Wales. He had also gained control of the estates of the Percy family in the north of England, while the heir was under-age.[6] Audley's marriage to Margaret of Clare, Gavaston's widow, similarly brought him large rewards. He received Tonbridge Castle in Kent, with various Clare manors throughout Kent, Surrey and Sussex. He also acquired Gwynllwg, which had formerly been part of Glamorgan, while the King's favour brought further rewards. The three men shared the Irish estates of the Clare family.[7] Montague, who became steward of the Household in 1316, used his influential position to advantage by arranging for his son to marry Joan, daughter of Theobald Verdon. The marriage took place in the chapel royal at Windsor, clear evidence of the King's favour.[8] The King's other supporters included the Earls of Hereford and Pembroke, Bartholomew Badlesmere, Henry Beaumont, John Giffard and John Cromwell, Keeper of the Tower of London. These men were close to the King and formed a group around him which excluded the Earl of Lancaster. The hapless Lancaster had clung stubbornly to the plan to restore lands granted by the King to their former holders, an idea that made him unpopular with the present owners, who had much to lose.

XVIII   THOMAS OF LANCASTER

Throughout 1317 the rift between Lancaster and the other Earls widened and at times verged on civil war. The Earl of Surrey went so far as to abduct Lancaster's wife and carry her off to his castle at Reigate in Surrey, possibly with the agreement of the King. Chroniclers suggest that she may have been happy with her fate and even embraced the man who carried her off.[1] The Pope's envoys arrived in England in the summer of 1317 in an attempt to make some kind of peace with both the Scots and with Lancaster. A meeting was organized at Nottingham for July 18th, but Lancaster failed to attend, setting out his reasons in a long letter.[2] He declared that his only aim was to uphold the King's peace and he kept a large retinue for this purpose, not, as was assumed, for opposing the King. He further claimed that ill-health prevented him from coming to Nottingham, but he may have been fearful of further plots against him, following the abduction of his wife.[3] He restated his arguments in his letter, pointing out that the King had failed to keep the conditions laid down in the Lincoln Parliament of 1316: he had not upheld the Ordinances; he had not consulted Parliament as he should have done; he had retained his favourites as 'evil counsellors' and his generosity to these men had endangered the rest of the country by depriving the Scottish campaign of financial support.

In addition to criticism in England, objections to the King's generosity to his close friends came from the Pope, who sent letters to Edward urging him to reduce his extravagance and be more careful about his choice of friends. He wrote, directing the King:

> To choose and retain counsellors able to rule his realm and to sit in his court when he cannot; to appoint judges and officials who shall not be venal; to lessen the expenses of his Household, so that he may be able to fulfil his purpose of assisting the Holy Land.

The Pope also wrote to various noblemen and associates of the King, such as Badlesmere and the Despensers, pleading with them to use their influence on the King to check his excessive financial demands on the clergy and to promote peace, both within England and with other countries.[4] There was a dramatic example of opposition to the King at the Whitsun festival in 1317. The King and Queen were dining in the banqueting-hall at Westminster when a woman in a mask, disguised as an entertainer, entered on horseback, rode up to the royal table and gave the King a letter. He assumed that it was part of the entertainment and, since he enjoyed the company of actors, he ordered it to be opened and read aloud to amuse the courtiers. However, the letter was a criticism of his qualities as King:

> The Lord King has failed to reward his knights who, during his father's reign and his own, have faced many dangers and have suffered either total or partial loss of their wealth, in proportion to their rank, while he has enriched others beyond reason, who have not yet taken up the burden of office.

The woman was at once arrested and confessed that she was acting on behalf of a certain knight. The knight acknowledged what he had done but said that he acted for the good of the realm and he assumed that the King would read the letter in private.[5] Much of the criticism of the King centred on his personal extravagance and his gifts to his friends at a time of great economic distress. As a way of easing some of the country's problems, Parliament had made a further attempt at price regulation, concentrating this time on the price of ale. Since ale was part of the daily diet of virtually everyone in the country, a price increase became a major grievance. The order related first to brewers in London and was then applied to the rest of the country, stating that, because of the bad weather and poor harvests over the previous two years, there was a shortage of wheat and barley. In view of the shortage, it was more important to use the grain for bread, leaving only the surplus for ale. Since this would result in a shortage of ale and an increase in costs, the prices for ale were fixed. For example, in London a gallon of better quality ale should be sold for one and half pence, while medium quality ale should retail at a gallon for one penny. Realistically, the prices were lower in market towns and in the countryside. Control of prices was left to the local officials where the ale was sold.[6]

Against this background of shortages and hardship, the King's extravagance provided a focus for criticism. The royal accounts included bills for expensive silks and cloth of gold for cushions for the carriages of the Queen and her ladies. The King ordered for himself six pairs of boots, with silk tassels and hanging decorations in silver gilt, at a cost of five shillings a pair. Edward and Isabella's gifts to courtiers were on a magnificent scale and the royal couple's fondness for music is reflected in the large sums of money paid to their musicians.[7] In addition, the King ordered a great new dining-table for Westminster Hall. There was also a lavish new tapestry for the walls, decorated with figures of the King and his nobles, being specially designed to be put up at the times of the great religious festivals. Because the tapestry was so valuable, a craftsman was employed to make a green border for it, both to protect the edges from damage and for fixing it to the wall.

As well as spending money, the King also received exotic presents and among the more unusual gifts was a pair of camels brought to the King by a servant of the Italian financier, Antony of Pessagno.[8] At about the same time Edward founded a society at Cambridge, later known as King's Hall, which was eventually incorporated into Trinity College. He gave money to buy law books and ordered the Exchequer to support a clerk and 12 children whom he sent to be educated there. The scholars were recruited from the chapel royal and were probably destined to be trained to work as officials within the Household. The following year, the Pope granted the foundation the full status of a university college.[9]

While many others lived in fear, the chief courtiers prospered; they formed a pact, sealed with a bond, by which Despenser the younger, Damory, Audley and Montague pledged sums of £6000 to one another. We do not know the aim of this agreement, but it shows a common purpose which united them in their opposition to Lancaster, and he responded with equal hostility.[10] The Earl's insistence that the King should restore lands to their former owners was at total variance to the intentions of the courtiers who held large estates by recent grants. Lancaster even refused to attend Parliament unless the courtiers were dimissed and, as a result, he was driven into opposition and isolation by his dedication to the Ordinances. Although the King granted him safe conduct to the meeting of Parliament in Lincoln, he refused to come, having been in fear for his life after his wife was taken.[11] In his absence and without his consent, Parliament proposed another Scottish campaign but, realistically, the country's finances could not afford it. The King attempted to remedy the lack of money by raising loans and he sent a deputation to the Pope, led by the Bishops of Ely and Norwich and the Earl of Pembroke, asking for yet another tax on the church.[12] In the meantime, he ordered his army to gather at York in preparation for the next Scottish war. He himself set out from London in July and stayed for a while at St Albans Abbey, where he blessed 22 sick people by touching them in the hope of healing them. He then travelled to Bedford, King's Cliffe in Northamptonshire and to Lincoln, eventually reaching York, where he stayed at the Convent of the Minor Friars. On the whole journey he blessed no less than 79 sick persons.[13]

Lancaster's men from the Yorkshire town of Pontefract blocked the way against the King's forces, on the grounds that Lancaster was steward of England, and any war-gathering needed his consent.[14] Lancaster's opposition to the King had driven him to make contact with the Scots and, with Scottish help, his men attacked and robbed Louis Beaumont, Bishop-elect of Durham, and his brother Henry, one of the King's close supporters, together with the two Cardinals, Gaucelin and Luke. The Cardinals, who had been sent to England by the Pope to negotiate peace between England and Scotland, were on their way to Durham for the consecration of Beaumont. Their presence brought additional problems, since the attack was meant to have been directed against the Beaumonts, not against them. They were soon released on the initiative of Lancaster, but their capture provided the Pope with further evidence of the King's lack of control. In addition, Lancaster, with the help of Scottish forces, laid siege to Damory's castles at Knaresborough in Yorkshire and Alton in Staffordshire, while he also threatened the Earl of Surrey's lands and castles in Yorkshire.

During these years, there were once again two rival courts, each determined to oppose the other; but neither was strong enough to overcome the other and the members of both travelled across the country, generally avoiding direct conflict. Other lords followed the examples of the King and Lancaster, each one safeguarding his own interests by force. However, open confrontation between the King and Lancaster now seemed inevitable. Edward organized his defences by handing over his castles to his trusted supporters: Pembroke took command of Berkhamsted Castle in Hertfordshire, Badlesmere was in charge of Leeds Castle in Kent, Despenser the younger held Odiham in Hampshire, and Ryvere, sheriff of the county of Gloucester, commanded the castle there. Similarly, Edward put 15 other castles on a war-footing. In the meantime, Lancaster remained in his castle at Pontefract.[15]

As the situation worsened, Pembroke, accompanied by Hereford and a group of churchmen, including the two Cardinals, met Lancaster at Pontefract, with the aim of averting civil war. This powerful assembly of negotiators managed to persuade Lancaster to agree to give up his attacks, to come to meetings of Parliament in peace and to show respect for the King. While he agreed to these terms, Lancaster once more reaffirmed his support for the Ordinances, which had the effect of antagonizing the King's supporters. The result was a truce, but only a temporary one. The King abandoned the proposed Scottish campaign for that year and moved south once more, spending Christmas at Westminster.

XIX   THE SIEGE OF BERWICK

General unrest in England had diverted the attention of the King and his nobles away from Scotland, giving Bruce a further chance to consolidate his position in the north. He had returned from Ireland, where his brother, Edward, had been helping the Irish chiefs to drive out the English settlers. But after Edward Bruce's defeat and death there, Robert once more focused his efforts on the north of England where the Scots had taken the town of Berwick and various English castles. They kept up the offensive and, advancing southwards into England, they almost reached Pontefract. The urgency of such a threat drove the English nobles to organize a meeting with Lancaster in April 1318. At this meeting, which was held in Leicester, the King's supporters agreed to uphold the Ordinances and to banish 'evil counsellors' from his presence. Furthermore, a compromise was reached over the question of the restoration of lands to former owners; it was decided that those who held the disputed lands should not benefit from them but should pay the profits to the Exchequer. In return for these concessions, Lancaster agreed to support the King. The nobles then left for London to discuss the proposals with the King when he returned from Windsor.

The agreement reached at Leicester formed the first step in a series of discussions which eventually led to a meeting between the King and Lancaster. However, one of the chief obstacles to such a meeting was the influence of the King's 'evil counsellors', identified principally as Audley, Damory, Despenser the elder and William Montague, who were the direct opponents of Lancaster and close companions of the King. Only their absence from court could persuade Lancaster to give his full support to the King. After two months of preliminary meetings and discussions following the Leicester agreement, the Bishops of Ely and Norwich met Lancaster at his castle at Tutbury in Staffordshire. Tutbury was one of Lancaster's chief holdings and he had earlier reconstructed the main gateway, making an impressive statement of his power. Finally, after a sequence of further tough negotiations, Lancaster came face to face with the King at Leake in Nottinghamshire, where the Treaty of Leake was framed in August 1318. Although this was just an outline settlement, it was enough to bring the two men together. They met a few days after the treaty was drawn up and exchanged the kiss of peace. Following the meeting, the details were worked out at a Parliament held at York in October. According to the terms of the treaty, the King's 'evil counsellors' were to be removed and replaced with an advisory council of nobles and churchmen. On the face of it, the King needed the consent of this council to rule but, in his typical fashion, he showed little interest in the arrangements. Audley, Damory and Montague left the court, but their place was soon taken by the younger Despenser, who eventually proved to be a far more dangerous enemy to the Ordainers than Damory and his friends.[1]

The treaty was finally ratified in Parliament, where the Ordinances were confirmed once again and, this time, Parliament took steps to enforce them. There was a review of the King's ministers in which those who were considered unsuitable were removed and replaced. In addition, the whole organization of the Household was put under scrutiny. The Household Ordinance of York, dated December 1318, drawn up by Badlesmere, Despenser the younger, Roger Northburgh and Gilbert Wigton, the four chief ministers of the Household, codified the arrangements. They listed every office and detailed the duties of that office, ranging from Treasurer and Chamberlain at the top to laundresses at the bottom. Such a careful scrutiny of offices was an attempt to exert control over the size and expenses of the Household and may have been deliberately intended to humiliate the King.[2]

In June 1318, Isabella had given birth to a daughter, at Woodstock near Oxford, in the house which was granted to her as part of her dower. This daughter was usually referred to as Eleanor of Woodstock, reflecting the importance of a large country house that was a favourite royal residence. Following the birth, the King made a gift of £333 to Isabella, to celebrate her churching feast.[3]

Although there was a certain level of agreement between the King and the Ordainers in 1318, it was too late in the year to begin another Scottish campaign and this was postponed until the following year. Bruce had already taken advantage of the preoccupations of the English nobility and was fortifying the northern towns and castles that he had captured. However, having gained the support of Lancaster, the King felt confident enough to plan a Scottish campaign for 1319. Edward left his half-brother, Thomas of Brotherton, who had been created Earl of Norfolk, as Keeper of the realm, and arrived at York early in 1319. Further taxation was imposed to bring in extra revenue to finance the war. Parliament met at York in May 1319 and the following weeks were spent preparing for the campaign. Troops were ordered to muster at Newcastle in July, where the King himself arrived in August, and his men were scheduled to be paid from August 1st. This campaign differed from earlier ones in that it had the consent of the Ordainers, and of Lancaster in particular. Edward led an impressively large army, which included the forces of Lancaster, Pembroke, Hereford, Audley, Damory and the younger Despenser. The army contained crossbowmen, English and Welsh archers, light-horsemen and knights with their retainers, and was supplemented by a sizeable contingent of sailors. As with earlier campaigns, most of the east coast ports of England provided ships and sailors for the war, carrying armaments as well as food. Since the King needed large amounts of ready cash for payments, Northburgh, Keeper of the Wardrobe, was made responsible for moving cash to the value of 4,000 marks from London to Berwick by land and water.

Having mustered at Newcastle, the army moved northwards. The first objective was the recapture of Berwick. This well-fortified town may have been betrayed and surrendered to the Scots by its English commander; certainly, its recapture proved to be far more difficult than Edward anticipated. Perhaps his decision to besiege the town was taken on the spur of the moment, since siege-engines and sappers had to be brought up from York Castle at short notice.[4] Having decided on a siege, the King optimistically declared that, now he had begun, he would stay until the town was taken and, as a further measure, he ordered another 100 sappers to be summoned from Holderness, on the east coast of Yorkshire. In addition, he sent orders to his Chancellor, who had remained at York, to organize a muster from the whole county and lead the men by night and day to Berwick, leaving the Great Seal at York for safe keeping. To enforce the order, the King declared that he had spies watching at all times to ensure that none could escape the muster.[5]

The English army attacked Berwick from the landward side, while the fleet also attempted an assault, but both were beaten back. John Barbour's poem, *The Bruce*, gives a fourteenth-century Scottish version of events. He describes how Walter the Steward, Bruce's son-in-law, was put in charge of the defence, assisted by archers, crossbowmen and 500 men-at-arms. There was a settlement of Flemish people in Berwick and Steward had the help of a Flemish engineer, John Crab, who made all kinds of engines of war, including springalds, missiles and cranes, but the defenders had no cannon. When Edward began his siege, the sea and river estuary were filled with his ships and so many English tents were pitched that they formed a tented town. As the attack was launched, the English advanced with banners flying; they carried ladders and scaffolding, pikes, shelters and the slings of siege-engines, all the apparatus for investing the town. As the trumpets sounded, the archers went first, then the attackers tried to place their ladders against the walls, but these were immediately thrown down. The lack of success led the English to bring a ship close up to the walls and they hauled a boat, full of armed men, half-way up its mast, but they could not come close enough to lay down a drawbridge into the town. As the tide went out, the ship ran aground and was burned by the Scots. Amid the fighting, the Scots captured an English engineer.

On the fifth day, Crab, the Flemish engineer, prepared a crane on wheels, which lowered burning faggots, pitch, tar and brimstone upon the attackers. They, in turn, prepared a 'sow', which was essentially a stout roof on wheels, pushed by the men inside it until it reached the town walls. With this as a protection, the English sappers could begin to undermine the walls. The Scots were prepared to set free the captured English engineer, on condition that he destroyed the sow. He followed their orders and placed a siege-engine opposite it, which fired shots that fell on the sow and crushed it. The men inside it rushed out in terror and the Scots delightedly cried out 'the sow has farrowed'. The English attacked repeatedly from their ships, from the topcastles (embattled platforms at the tops of the masts) and from boats hauled up the masts to overtop the walls. From these high positions, the archers fired down on the garrison, but they could not take the town. Finally, they withdrew and Bruce sent for masons to build the walls higher as a protection against further attacks.[6]

Chroniclers laid the blame for failure on the King and his 'usual stupidity', reflecting on the weakness of character of a King who reacted to failure by motivating his supporters with promises of wealth to come.[7] For example, he promised Despenser the younger and Damory that they would have both the castle and the town of Berwick, when victory was won. The chroniclers recorded how he made encouraging promises to such low people as 'despicable idlers', telling them how much they would gain from success, while treating his nobles with contempt. Old scores still rankled with him and he swore to avenge the murder of Gavaston. His attitude served only to increase Lancaster's unease and the Earl withdrew his men from the siege.[8]

Isabella had accompanied her husband on his northward journey and, while he went on to Berwick, she remained with her children at Brotherton, near Pontefract, in the place where her aunt, Queen Margaret, had stayed when Edward I was campaigning in Scotland. Isabella chose Brotherton for her home, thinking this was a place of comparative safety, nearly 100 miles from the war zone. But her security was threatened as the Earl of Douglas was marching southwards into England in her direction. However, one of his men was caught and, when he was taken before the Archbishop of York, he disclosed Douglas' plan to capture the Queen and the royal children. Although the King's ministers at York were at first sceptical about the threat to the Queen, they brought her to York for safety and then transferred her by boat to Nottingham.[9]

Men from York, led by the Archbishop, then encountered the advancing Scottish soldiers who fought a hard battle and took many English prisoners, retreating with them towards the Border. In the meantime, the English attack on Berwick had failed once more. The structures, which had been designed to protect the sappers while they were undermining the walls, were destroyed, the besiegers were beaten back and the English fleet was under attack.[10] When Edward heard the news of Douglas' attempt to capture the Queen, he called a council of war. His advisers gave conflicting advice; those who had been offered the spoils of Berwick wanted to stay and take the town, while others, whose lands were threatened by the Scottish army, wished to leave the town to protect their possessions. The Lanercost chronicler recorded that the King was hoping to divide his forces, so that he could accommodate both groups.[11] In the event, he abandoned the siege after ten days and turned to face the Scottish army as it moved northwards from Yorkshire. The evidence of the chronicles suggests that Edward would have preferred to stay and take Berwick since he had invested such a huge effort in setting up the siege. Also, the town was of strategic importance and its capture would have brought him great prestige. But the Earl of Lancaster took the opposite view and there were rumours that he was acting with the connivance of the Scots.[12] Certainly, he left Berwick, taking his men with him, claiming that he needed to protect his own land from the Scottish army. In addition, Edward's plan to intercept the Scots as they returned to their homeland failed, since they had already escaped by taking the western route, by way of Carlisle.[13] The King returned to Newcastle and then gloomily moved south to York, leaving Badlesmere in Newcastle to organize the security of the Border castles.

While the military campaign was unsuccessful, the King did not lack diversions. His musicians, notably 'King' Robert, received considerable rewards, as did two minstrels of the King of France. Hunting also helped to pass the time. He sent huntsmen to Wales to bring back hunting-dogs, and two of his falcons were brought from London, one called Beaumont and the other Damory, after two of his favourite courtiers.[14] The King made his headquarters at York, where the clerks of the Exchequer had set up their office, bringing cartloads of documents with them from London.[15] The fortifications of the city were strengthened and the royal party, which included his friends, Beaumont, Despenser the younger and Pembroke, was protected by a large force of armed men. Although Edward remained in the north, it proved difficult for him to organize further expeditions against the Scots without Lancaster's co-operation. In addition to concerns about Scotland, he was faced with demands from Philip V, the new King of France, who had succeeded his brother Louis X, that he should go to

France to perform homage for the English lands in Gascony. These extra demands forced him to make a truce with the Scots which was intended to last for two years, giving him time to visit France and perhaps gather another army for a future Scottish expedition. He then left York and travelled southwards, as the chronicler put it, in a rather aimless way, lacking the glory and dignity that might be expected of a King of England. Predictably, there were accusations that he was a slave to idleness and did not care for glory, fame or noble deeds on a royal scale.[16] The chronicler of the *Life of Edward II* suggests that the truce was unwelcome to some of the English nobles, because they felt it was degrading to the King but, without the support of Lancaster, he had no alternative. There are also hints that his heart was not in the siege of Berwick, since he was still deeply affected by the death of Gavaston. He had certainly not forgotten his friend and the accounts for the year include payments for a turquoise cloth to cover Gavaston's body in the chapel at Langley.[17] Lancaster's unwillingness to co-operate and the differences of opinion among the nobles contributed to the King's lack of success, principally because he did not have the ability, or even the inclination, either to assert his will or to plan effectively.

On his return from the north, Edward looked for a refuge in London and chose a building, described as a hut (*tugurrium*), within the precincts of Westminster Abbey, which was known by the name of 'Burgundy'. He took this over and began to build there, 'preferring to be called King of Burgundy, instead of using the magnificent titles of his famous royal ancestors'.[18] This follows his earlier action of taking over a manor-house at Westminster that belonged to the Abbey, which he then used as a country retreat.[19] Although his withdrawal from political life aroused both criticism and surprise, he chose to follow a path that pleased him, seeking relief from war and politics.

XX RECONCILIATION

A meeting of Parliament was called at York in January 1320, but Lancaster refused to attend what he described as 'a secret meeting', since it was not a meeting for the whole of Parliament. He persisted with his intention that the country should be governed openly 'by consent'.[1] During this time the King was relying increasingly on the support and guidance of William Stapledon, Bishop of Exeter, whom he regarded as his trusted friend and adviser. He relied on the Bishop to such an extent that he appointed him Treasurer of the Exchequer in place of Walter of Norwich. The King went further in making appointments independently, without the consent of Parliament, giving Badlesmere the office of steward of the Household and making Despenser the younger his Chamberlain, a position which gave him control over the officials of the Household and over access to the King. It is noteworthy that Gavaston had once held the same office.[2]

It soon became necessary for Edward to go to France to do homage to Philip V for his lands in France. His visit was first planned to take place in March 1320, but it was postponed for a while and the King spent a month travelling through Kent, returning to London in April. It eventually took place in June and he appointed Pembroke to be Keeper of the realm during his absence, which lasted for just over a month. Damory was once more at the forefront of events, accompanying the King and Queen to France, together with Despenser the younger and the Bishops of Norwich and Exeter. Others, including Despenser the elder, Badlesmere and Edmund of Woodstock, the King's half-brother, joined the royal party after they arrived in France. The King and Queen went to Amiens and Edward did homage for his French lands. Apart from the Earl of Pembroke, the whole court was in France for this month.[3] After the month's absence, the citizens of London gave the King a warm welcome on his return. 'The Mayor and citizens rode out and, dressed in clothes appropriate to their office, they advanced to meet him in fine style'.[4]

In contrast with the elaborate reception given to Edward by the Londoners and perhaps as a sign of discontent with the King's behaviour, an imposter had appeared at Oxford. The man claimed to be the true surviving son of Edward I and Queen Eleanor, saying that the present King was the son of a carter who had tricked his way into the Household to make love to the Queen. The people of Oxford sent the young man to the King at Northampton, where he was questioned and hanged for claiming to be King, as an example to any other possible pretenders. In another version of the same story, the pretender-King, whose face was scarred, declared that, when he was a baby, he had been so badly savaged by a voracious pig, that the royal nurse had hidden him away and substituted the child of a carter of the same age. As further proof of his case, he asserted that Edward's low birth was clearly responsible for his vulgar and rustic interests.[5]

During the early months of 1320 both the Despensers were active on the King's behalf. As we have seen, both were at the court of the King of France, while the elder Despenser had also been at the papal court at Avignon. Edmund of Woodstock led this embassy to the Pope, which may have had the appointment of Badlesmere's nephew as Bishop of Lincoln as its ostensible objective. But there are suggestions that behind the scenes lay the King's wish to gain the support of the Pope in order to absolve him from his oath to maintain the Ordinances.[6] The Despensers, Badlesmere, Robert Baldock and the Bishop of Exeter were the men who now had the ear of the King, while Lancaster distanced himself from the court and remained isolated in the north, probably at his castle at Pontefract. After returning from France, the King seemed to be at peace with himself and his associates, who appear to have exerted some good influence on him. There were favourable comments about improvements in his behaviour and he even banned from court various companies of entertainers who annoyed people with their excessive rudeness and greed.[7] He was amiable during the meeting of Parliament at Westminster, making grants at the request of the Ordainers and with the agreement of Parliament.[8] The Bishop of Worcester went so far as to comment on the change in the King, who got up early and took part amenably in parliamentary business. In a letter to Cardinal Vitalis he described the King as behaving 'respectfully, wisely and with discernment, listening patiently to all who wished to speak to him'. As a result, people began to look for a permanent change in his character, hoping that he would incline more to peace and unity.[9] He also dealt sensibly with matters relating to the poor and showed mercy or severity, as appropriate, in judicial cases, much to the surprise of those who were present.[10] The atmosphere of conciliation continued and there was no evidence of opposition from the Ordainers when Despenser the younger was made constable of Bristol and Badlesmere became constable of Dover. Even the King's various advisers seemed to be at peace with one another.[11] However, this time of peace did not last and, in spite of the outward appearance of harmony, another crisis began to develop, arising mainly from the ambitions of the younger Despenser and his influence over the King. The extent of Despenser's power stirred up differences among the nobles and eventually forced Lancaster to take action.

XXI   REBELLION IN WALES

The most powerful of the Lords of the Welsh Marches had been Gilbert of Clare, Earl of Gloucester, but the long period of his minority and his early death at Bannockburn had left the Marches in an unsettled state. Despenser the younger had already acquired large Clare estates in south Wales through his marriage with Eleanor of Clare, Gilbert's sister. Following his marriage, Despenser had increased his holdings by obtaining further grants from the King, which included full sovereignty throughout the county of Glamorgan.[1] By an exchange of lands with Audley, he had gained control of the town and castle of Newport, together with much of the surrounding land. The modern castle is low-lying and close to the River Usk, but the medieval structure lay in a prominent position on the top of a hill, overlooking the town, with a commanding view of the bridge over the Usk.[2] All this had been part of the Clare inheritance which Audley had acquired by marriage and was now in the hands of Despenser. He also tried to increase the profitability of his estates by locating the staple of wool at Cardiff. (Certain ports were classified as staples where merchants paid money to allow them to trade and where customs dues were collected).[3] At the same time, Despenser began the process of acquiring Lundy Island, which would give him control over the Bristol Channel. He followed this by trying to take over the Gower peninsula, which adjoined his lands in Glamorgan. While enjoying the position at court once held by Gavaston, he was also attempting to set up a huge territorial power base in south Wales, stretching from Pembrokeshire in the west to the eastern border of Monmouthshire. Furthermore, in his capacity as Chamberlain to the King, he was able to promote his own supporters to high office. Among these was Robert Baldock, an official of the Household, who later acted as the King's Chancellor. While in office, he remained 'the brain and hand of the younger Despenser'.

However, other lords challenged Despenser's claim to Gower. The claimants were: John Mowbray, who was son-in-law to William Broase, the Lord of Gower, secondly, the Earl of Hereford, who claimed it for his son, Edward, and finally, Roger Mortimer, Lord of Chirk and Justice of all Wales, and his nephew, Roger Mortimer of Wigmore. Mowbray took the initiative by seizing Swansea Castle and claiming the lordship of Gower. In reply, Despenser persuaded the King to take over Gower, on the grounds that Mowbray had acted illegally. But the King's seizure of Gower was regarded by the other lords of the Welsh Marches as a sign of Despenser's ambition and they united in their hatred of the Despensers. As a measure to calm the fears of the Marcher Lords, who included Audley, the Mortimers, Roger Clifford and Damory, the King confirmed his father's grants to Gilbert of Clare in 1290. This was intended to show Audley and Damory, who had married the other Clare heiresses, that Despenser would not lay claim to their share of the Clare inheritance.[4] However, these men and others were suspicious of the Despensers and resented their control over the King. The power of the younger Despenser aroused fear in others, since 'he was the King's right eye, but an eye-sore to the rest of the kingdom. His every desire became a royal command'.[5] In the same way as Gavaston had dealt with business on the King's behalf, only the Despensers now had access to the King. A chronicler referred to the 'great schism' that arose between the King and his lords because of his great affection for the younger Despenser. There were complaints that he high-handedly dismissed other office-holders and put his own men in their place without consultation. Fierce anger surged up among the great men of the country against this man who was 'fired by greed' and could dominate the King and lead him on, as if he were 'teasing a cat with a piece of straw'.[6]

Once again, civil war threatened, directed this time against Despenser. Badlesmere, who had now become Edward's confidential agent, was sent to negotiate an extended truce with the Scots, since the King could not maintain a war on two fronts. On the other hand, the Marcher Lords, led by the Earl of Hereford, appealed to Lancaster for help, in his capacity as Lord of Kidwelly, which lies to the north-west of the Gower peninsula. The threat of such powerful opposition spurred the King to act in defence of the Despensers. On March 1st 1321, he sent orders from Westminster to his official, Robert Woodhouse, to review his castles in Wales, to check their supplies and prepare them for war. Edward followed these commands with further instructions from Sheen, in Surrey, on March 3rd, with orders to make his castles defensible and, in particular, to ensure that every castle was provided with two barrels of honey (honey, can be mixed with sulphur and saltpetre to form gunpowder). Edward then moved on to Windsor, from where he sent instructions to the Abbot of Glastonbury to provide him with a loan from the taxation levied on the clergy. There were further orders to the sheriffs of Gloucestershire, Somerset and Dorset to send supplies of wheat and beans to Caernarvon Castle to feed the occupying garrison, while Despenser the younger, or his deputy, as keeper of Bristol, was ordered to supply the honey for the Welsh castles.[7] Edward left Windsor and made his way westwards, going first to

Gloucester to take precautions against the coming storm. Having reached the city, he concentrated on fortifying the gateways, doors, bridges and walls of the castle. He also strengthened the garrison at Newport Castle. He took the castle of St Briavels from Damory and issued an order for the confiscation of Audley's estates. Furthermore, he took over Montgomery Castle and then returned to Gloucester. From there, he went to Bristol and spent Easter at Bristol Castle, which he left fully provisioned when he returned to London on May 5th.

During these months there had been no open conflict as messages and orders flew between the King's advisers and their opponents, without any decisions being taken. There was already plenty of hostility to the Despensers in Wales because of the part they had played in the unjustified execution of Llewellyn Bren and, when the King departed for London, the Marcher Lords reacted with force and began to lay waste the Despenser lands in Wales. They made a united attack throughout Glamorgan in the early months of 1321. On May 4th, they rode first towards Newport with an army of 1,300 mounted men and 10,000 men on foot, carrying the royal coat-of-arms before them as a sign of their loyalty to the Crown. After a siege lasting for four days, they captured both the town and the castle, and then went on to ransack the surrounding lands. Their attack severely damaged the castle, which was afterwards restored to Audley for reconstruction. An order for 300 oak trees for the repairs gives some idea of the extent of the damage.[8] On the following Saturday, they took Cardiff Castle and then attacked the massive stronghold of Caerphilly Castle, which was garrisoned by Despenser's men. They expelled the keeper and took possession. This was quickly followed by the capture of castles at Swansea and Loughor. In a further series of attacks lasting almost a week, they took over other Despenser lands and then went on to devastate various Despenser estates in Gloucestershire. The chronicler of the *Life of Edward II* emphasizes the general hatred towards the Despensers, which led the lords to take any revenge they could, while claiming to be acting on behalf of the King:

> They rode the length of England, displaying the banner of the Lord King; and so they went from place to place, where the Despensers, father and son, held property, and installed new keepers and bailiffs, acting for the King.[9]

The official records reveal the extent of opposition to the Despensers, listing their main enemies as the Earl of Hereford, the Mortimers, Audley, Maurice Berkeley and Damory and adding many more. There are details of how the Marchers ransacked the Despenser lands, stealing their possessions, burning documents, destroying ten castles in Wales and causing similar damage in England. The description of the damage only emphasized the wealth of the Despensers, who lost possessions which were luxurious on a royal scale, such as tables of ivory and ebony, chessboards with crystal chessmen, silver, jewellery and clothes, all of great value.[10]

Edward was faced with a massive revolt and he called a meeting of advisers. Again he received conflicting views, as some urged him to go to war against the Marcher Lords, while others felt that such a war would ruin the country and advised him to hold a meeting of Parliament at Westminster, so that complaints could be properly heard. The King's opponents agreed to come to such a meeting, but they came with their private armies. There was no chance of reaching any agreement in a situation where the Marchers claimed to be acting for the King against the Despensers, while Edward was trying desperately to protect his friends. He attempted to save them by his usual method of employing delaying tactics and he kept up lengthy negotiations in London.[11] At the same time, in order to strengthen his military position further, the King sent Badlesmere to Wales to check the fortifications and military equipment at Montgomery Castle. However, Badlesmere unexpectedly defected and joined the Marcher Lords. While there is no direct evidence for his sudden change of heart, he may have felt threatened by the increasing power of the Despensers, since he, too, held lands in the Marches of Wales.[12] Whatever his reasons may have been, he now committed his support to the Marcher Lords.

During this time, Lancaster had been organizing meetings of his supporters in Yorkshire, at Pontefract and Sherburn-in-Elmet. While such meetings might reflect general anxiety about attacks by the Scots on northern England, the presence of the Lords of the Welsh Marches probably indicates a wider aim and Lancaster may have been trying to revive the Ordinances, with the intention of using them to destroy the Despensers. There was the familiar emphasis on the removal of 'evil counsellors', who attended the King and gave him bad advice and, while the Despensers were not named, the reference to giving the King bad advice was probably directed at them.[13] The Lords of the Marches then gathered their retinues and moved southwards. When they reached the outskirts of London, they divided their forces; the Mortimers took up residence at the Hospital of St John at Clerkenwell, the headquarters of the Knights Hospitallers, Hereford was at Holborn, in a house belonging to Lancaster, Damory was at the New Temple and Audley stayed at the Priory of St Bartholomew, in Smithfield. The other leaders and their forces stayed nearby. There were protracted negotiations as the Archbishop of Canterbury and various Bishops hurried to and fro, attempting to mediate between the King and his opponents. Hereford asked for a meeting with city leaders so that he could explain the reason for the presence of their armies. The meeting took place at Holborn, at Lancaster's house, where the Earl put the case that they had come to protect the King and the kingdom from the Despensers and their accomplices, who were traitors to both King and kingdom. He also asserted that the Despensers had taken the Tower of London and were intending to destroy the city. The citizens then asked for time to consider the situation. At about the same time, they also sent a deputation to the King, who characteristically kept them waiting for a reply. When he eventually replied, he urged them not to support his opponents and declared that his aim was to destroy all his enemies, 'even if they were his father or his son'. Faced with such conflicting demands, the citizens put their own interests first and decided not to support either side, but to concentrate on defending London against any form of attack.

The King reacted typically by maintaining his reluctance to hold meetings with his opponents or to take any specific action, in the hope that the situation would resolve itself. In the meantime, Despenser the younger kept a large contingent of armed men aboard a warship on the Thames near Gravesend, and was able to contact the King by river. The Marcher Lords, angry with the King's slow reactions, threatened to set fire to buildings extending from Charing Cross as far as the monastery where they believed Despenser was secretly meeting him. The King's failure to act even drove them to take the unprecedented step of threatening him with deposition, declaring they would put up another King who would rule with greater justice. Finally, in the face of open confrontation, mediators were forced to come forward. These included the Earl of Pembroke, who had recently returned from abroad, the Earl of Richmond, the Archbishop of Canterbury and various leading churchmen. Queen Isabella also joined them and, in a concerted effort, they persuaded the King to accept the Ordinances. At a meeting in Westminster Hall, Edward, accompanied by Pembroke and Richmond, reluctantly agreed to the demands of his opponents. The main force of their hostility was directed against the Despensers, who were accused of greed and treachery and of being enemies to King and country. They charged the two men with controlling access to the King, refusing admittance to other advisers, appointing their own supporters to be sheriffs of counties and constables of castles and causing commissioners, who were ignorant of the law, to make enquiries, to hear and determine cases *(oyer et terminer)*, with the result that innocent people were punished and their lands confiscated. Furthermore, they accused the Despensers of causing a war for their own purposes, seizing royal power and refusing to allow churchmen to speak to the King without payment. Both men were found guilty and were banished, in a way that mirrored the banishment of Gavaston.[14]

While some leading churchmen agreed with the banishment order, the Bishop of Exeter and several other Bishops were unwilling to give total support to the expulsion of the Despensers. Nevertheless, Despenser the elder immediately went to France, while his son stayed at sea, remaining close to the coast of Kent. On the King's orders, he was put under the protection of the sailors of the Cinque Ports and, instead of disappearing into exile, he acted like 'a sea-monster, trapping the merchants who crossed his path'. Among others, he captured a great merchant ship from Italy and took all the treasure he found on board. According to a chronicler, he terrorized the seas off the east coast, capturing the goods of Englishmen and foreigners alike.[15]

Although the King was now almost without supporters, in a reaction that was typical of his character, he chose to ignore the demands of the Ordainers. He had never intended to accept a decision that he had made under duress and he was soon in communication with Despenser the younger, the two men plotting to overturn the banishment order. The Marcher Lords, to a certain extent, had played into the King's hands for, by destroying and laying waste the Despenser lands, they had acted contrary to their own stated aim, which was the restoration of this property to the Crown. Therefore, the recovery of this property by the King could be defined as a legitimate act. Higden, in his *Polychronicon*, painted a doleful picture of the country at this time: ruled by a feeble King, while the Lords of the Marches engineered the exile of the Despensers and destroyed their castles in Wales, taking their animals and goods and occupying the city of Gloucester. But Higden also related how the King found a way to recall his friends from exile without consulting Parliament, 'which caused great strifes and debate'.[16]

An opportunity for Edward to take action came in October 1321, after he had ordered Badlesmere, his former steward, to give up his offices as constable of Dover Castle and keeper of Tonbridge Castle, following his desertion to join the Marcher Lords. Badlesmere immediately put his castles of Leeds and nearby Chilham, both in Kent, on a war-footing, and went to join the Marchers who were at Oxford. In the meantime, the King and Queen went on a pilgrimage to the shrine of St Thomas Becket at Canterbury. Edward then left Canterbury and travelled to the Isle of Thanet, where he had arranged a meeting with Despenser the younger. The Queen, however, was intending to stay at Leeds Castle on her return journey. There had been an earlier castle at Leeds, which had been very much altered during the reign of Edward I; it was held by Queen Eleanor and then by her successor, Queen Margaret. In effect, it was Isabella's own castle, since it had passed to her after the death of Queen Margaret, but it was placed in the keepership of Badlesmere. She had sent advance notice of her plan to stay at the castle so that preparations could be made for her visit. Badlesmere, who was absent at the time, had left his wife in charge and she refused to let anyone enter without permission from her husband. The Queen herself asked to be admitted, but even her personal request was refused and she had to find another lodging for the night. She then complained to the King that she had been refused entry to her own castle. There is a suggestion that the King deliberately engineered the situation, knowing that the Queen would be barred from entry. In this way, he could justify taking revenge on a man whom he had once trusted as his true friend and confidential agent.[17]

A secret meeting was organized between Edward's two half-brothers, Thomas, Earl of Norfolk, and Edmund of Woodstock, who had been created Earl of Kent, and the Earls of Arundel, Pembroke, Surrey and others. They declared their support for the King, gathered an army, mainly consisting of Londoners, and laid siege to the castle. The Lords of the Marches assembled at Kingston-upon-Thames, in Surrey, and considered what action to take. However, they received a message from Lancaster suggesting that they should not intervene to help Badlesmere, who was in the unfortunate position of having antagonized both sides. He had first deserted Lancaster and the Ordainers to support the King and then deserted Edward. As a result, he received no help from either side and Leeds Castle soon fell. Badlesmere's other castles were also taken, together with all the remaining possessions of the Earl of Hereford, Damory and Audley.[18]

XXII DEATH OF THOMAS OF LANCASTER

The King's successful action at this time had the effect of draining support away from Lancaster and Edward now saw his chance to bring back the Despensers. He ordered Archbishop Reynolds to summon an assembly of clergy in London to discuss revoking the banishment order. At this assembly, held in St Paul's Cathedral on December 1st 1321, the Earls of Arundel and Richmond and Robert Baldock presented the protest of the Despensers against their exile. The protest disputed the legality of the banishment order, particularly since it did not have the overwhelming support of the clergy. The Earls of Arundel, Pembroke and Richmond then declared that they had consented to the exile of the Despensers, but only under duress, out of fear of what the Marcher Lords might do.[1] Edward followed this up and, on December 7th, he summoned various clergymen, nobles and justices to him individually in the Green Chamber at Westminster Palace and asked each one whether the banishment order was unlawful. They all agreed with him that it was unlawful and, on December 8th, Despenser the younger was offered protection.[2]

The King had cleverly and successfully used the decision of the church assembly as a substitute for the consent of Parliament.[3] He took immediate action to recover the lands taken by the Marcher Lords and led his forces towards the Welsh Marches, spending Christmas at Cirencester, not far from Gloucester, a city which the Marchers had taken from the Despensers and fortified against them.[4] At Shrewsbury on January 15th 1322, he ordered the constable of Bristol, or his deputy, to arrest the two Mortimers, Audley, Damory and many others.[5] At this stage, the Mortimers surrendered to the King, who sent them to the Tower of London. Other Marcher Lords went to join Lancaster, who was then in Yorkshire at his castle of Pontefract. The King took advantage of their departure and was able to recover the city of Gloucester. He also took over Berkeley Castle after the surrender and arrest of Maurice Berkeley. Edward then set off for Coventry, following the route taken by his opponents, and went on to Nottingham and then Burton-upon-Trent, in Staffordshire, still in pursuit. He had planned to stay at Burton, but his men were driven back by the enemy who held the bridge over the River

Trent. Finally, by March 10th, he crossed the river and reached Tutbury, where he took both the town and the castle, formerly held by Lancaster. After the attack, Edward met Roger Damory on his deathbed, a man who had once been one of his closest friends but died his enemy.

In the meantime, the Queen had ordered supplies to be sent to York and Carlisle for the King's use. In the event, the armies of the King and the rebels met at Boroughbridge, in Yorkshire, on March 16th 1322. As the rebels were attempting to move northwards to seek Scottish support, they were intercepted by Andrew Harclay, sheriff of Cumberland, in a battle that lasted from midday until sunset. The Earl of Hereford was killed and the rebel army was scattered in defeat. The next day, Lancaster was captured near Pontefract and was taken to the King at Pontefract Castle. The King's Justices, the Earls of Pembroke and Richmond, and the two Despensers, who had returned to England in the meantime, condemned him to death as a traitor. He was tied to a mule but, being of royal blood, he was beheaded rather than having to suffer the final degradation of being drawn and hanged. By executing Lancaster, who had killed Gavaston, Edward had the satisfaction of avenging the death of his great friend.[6] Following the battle, many others, including Badlesmere, were caught and put to death. The death of Lancaster made the man into a martyr. An anthem was composed, comparing him with Thomas Becket, 'whose head was broken because of the peace of the Church and his (Lancaster's) was cut off for the cause of peace in England'.[7] Great crowds of people flocked to visit his tomb at Pontefract, where many miracles supposedly occurred, and a chapel was later erected to mark the place of his execution. He had once been the richest landowner in the country, apart from the King, and had been regarded by many as the potential saviour of the kingdom.[8]

After the battle at Boroughbridge, Parliament was summoned to York on May 2nd. At this meeting, the banishment order against the Despensers was formally revoked and the Ordinances of 1311 were officially repealed, on the grounds that they were illegal and limited the powers of the Crown. However, the principle of having Ordinances was not abandoned totally and some were retained, but in a different form. Nine Ordinances were made by the King, with the agreement of Parliament, and six of these were redrafted forms of the original Ordinances of 1311. The session at York established the principle that Parliament was a place of debate, where the King held the overriding power of veto. The year 1322 marked a dramatic change. For a brief time, the King regained his royal power. His enemies were either dead or in prison and their estates were under his control. The rebellion and the battle at Boroughbridge had removed about 118 nobles and other landowners; it effectively wiped out opposition to the King for the time being. The economic situation had improved because of better harvests and a fall in the prices of foodstuffs. In addition, the truce with Scotland had eased the burden of taxation throughout the country. For once, Edward had acted with vigour in pressing the attack against the rebels and this forceful policy had brought numerous supporters to his cause, with the result that Lancaster had been isolated, made vulnerable and then disposed of. But the Despensers were now in the ascendant; Higden recorded, 'from that time the power of the Despensers began to increase and the power of the Queen decreased'.[9]

XXIII   THE RETURN OF THE DESPENSERS

While the armies of the King and Lancaster were in conflict at Boroughbridge, the Queen was in the safety of the Tower of London where she gave birth to a daughter, who became known as Joan of the Tower. Isabella may have been safe in the Tower but she was hardly comfortable, as rain poured in through the roof and on to her bed while she was giving birth.[1] Sometime before the birth, the two Mortimers, uncle and nephew, were placed in the Tower, following their surrender to the King. They were both under arrest and sentenced to death, like many others, for their opposition to the territorial ambitions of the Despensers in Wales and the Welsh Marches. Mortimer the elder died in prison from starvation and neglect, but his nephew, Roger Mortimer of Wigmore, being younger, had a stronger physique which enabled him to survive. For some reason, the death sentence on him was commuted into life imprisonment in the Tower. There are uncorroborated suspicions that this may have been due to the intervention of the Queen who was at the Tower while Mortimer was imprisoned there. Certainly, his reprieve was unusual in view of his great hostility to the Despensers. It was an act of mercy by the King which had dangerous consequences for him.[2]

The victory at Boroughbridge had brought the courtiers, headed by the Despensers, to great power. The Despensers, in particular, continued to acquire more lands and more honours. During the meeting of Parliament at York in 1322 the elder Despenser was created Earl of Winchester, while his son received many of the estates of the defeated Marcher Lords. Between 1322-6 the younger Despenser recovered all the lands he had lost at the time of his banishment and added many more. Following the death of Damory and the imprisonment of Audley, he took over their shares of the Clare inheritance, while further grants from the King placed many other estates under his control. At the same time, the elder Despenser acquired additional lordships, so that almost all of south Wales became Despenser territory.[3] As a clear mark of royal favour, when Despenser the younger regained possession of his castle at Hanley, in Worcestershire, which had been extensively plundered by his enemies, the King paid for most of the restoration work, but it went far beyond mere restoration and involved major rebuilding, making the castle 'the finest in the land'. It was also notable that the King's carpenters received a bonus payment for their efforts, 'in the presence of the King and the Lord Hugh'.[4] There is no direct evidence of a homosexual relationship between these two men; nevertheless, Despenser the younger had acquired the same dominating influence over the King once possessed by Gavaston, and homosexuality was probably the binding element within the King's circle of friends. Through his friendship with the King, Despenser the younger was now more powerful than ever. In his capacity as Chamberlain of the Household, he controlled access to the King and demanded payments from petitioners who wished for royal favours. Money also flowed in from his estates, which he increased all the time, sometimes even resorting to criminal methods, such as kidnapping and imprisoning an heiress until her estates were handed over to him. With this level of income, Despenser was able to provision his castles, to build a great new ship called *La Despenser* and pay for a lavish way of life as he travelled through his vast estates. In addition, he was able to deposit large amounts of money with Italian bankers for safekeeping. The bankers operated in England, France and the Netherlands and managed his income and expenditure reliably and efficiently, paying out the money to equip his castles and settling his bills for expensive clothes and silver plate, as well as for many other minor items. Under the supervision of the Chamber office, headed by the Chamberlain, some of the King's favourite residences, including those at Byfleet and Sheen in Surrey, at Gravesend and Strood in Kent, at Windsor Park, Kenilworth Castle, at Adderley in Shropshire, once held by Badlesmere, and, above all, Langley, were managed by men who were his personal servants. With this kind of arrangement, the King could relax and enjoy himself at his favourite houses, surrounded by congenial companions. The revenues that came into the Chamber paid for his personal expenses such as, gifts, jewellery and gambling debts.[5]

While the Despensers flourished, the fortunes of the defeated rebels, sometimes known as the Contrariants, faded. Their extensive estates were now in the hands the Crown. The lands ranged across the country from Cornwall to Essex and from Surrey in the south to County Durham and Yorkshire in the north. They included the five earldoms once held by Thomas of Lancaster and the estates of many other Contrariants, as well as some of the former Templar lands which had not yet been handed over to the Knights Hospitallers. Not only the lands of many of the Contrariants now belonged to the King, but many of their personal possessions also flowed into his Treasury. These included a gold cup, bearing the coat-of-arms of Audley, silver dishes, cups and spoons from the collections of the elder Mortimer and of many others. In all, by the victory at

Boroughbridge, the Exchequer had acquired control of extensive financial and military resources. If these resources had been efficiently exploited, they would have greatly improved the financial position of the King but, in reality, many of the estates were neglected and the revenues were never fully collected. In spite of various attempts to regulate the management of finance by officials of the Exchequer, expenditure invariably exceeded income. A typical account roll for Gloucestershire for 1321-22 listed the lands which were then taken over by the King and it presented a dismal picture, showing lack of investment, general depression and very little income. This situation was repeated in many other areas. An additional effect of the forfeiture of the estates of the Contrariants was a great increase in government administration and bureaucracy to deal with the management of all the property. The amount of documentation was tripled or even quadrupled, in some cases, and extra clerks had to be employed to handle the work of record-keeping. This growth in bureaucracy was also a severe drain on the administration and finances of the Church, since many of the clerks in royal service were absentee clergymen who continued to be supported by the Church.[6]

Once again the Scots began to present problems for England. The two-year truce made with Bruce had expired and he organized yet another campaign of raids into northern England in 1322. Edward wrote to the Pope, to various Cardinals and other leading figures abroad, informing them about the latest Scottish invasions, and once again he summoned his army to muster at Newcastle.[7] At the same time, he ordered the Exchequer to move from Westminster to York to be near him during the campaign. It so happens that this journey has been well-documented and we can see, in detail, how the move was arranged. Orders were sent to the sheriff of Yorkshire and the officials of the city of York telling them to make ready both the castle and the houses that had been used by the royal party on previous occasions. Responsibility for any expenditure lay with the sheriff, who was informed that he could later recoup his outlay from the Exchequer. The date set for the move was April 5th 1322. First of all, the clerks had to sort out the records and decide which to take and which to leave behind. When they had made their decisions, they bought empty wine casks that had to be cleaned, mended and lined with waxed canvas. They packed the documents into the wine casks, which were then loaded on to carts. The luggage also included chests full of money and treasure. In all, there were about 23 carts, each one drawn by five horses, and about 50 officials travelling with the convoy, protected by a contingent of men on foot and on horseback. They stayed first at Cheshunt, in Hertfordshire, and spent the Easter weekend at Grantham, in Lincolnshire. Next they went to Lincoln, then Torksey, from where they travelled by water along the River Trent to Burton-upon-Stather, where they had to stay longer than anticipated because of storms and floods. Eventually, they arrived at York and settled in their quarters in the castle, after a journey lasting thirteen days. Although moving government departments in this way might be slow and inconvenient, it was useful for the King to have them fairly near at hand, rather than having to rely on extended and precarious lines of communication with Westminster.[8]

The King's Wardrobe accounts for 1322 reveal the economic effects of such a Scottish expedition on the whole country. Huge amounts of provisions poured into Newcastle, which was the main supply-base for castles at Bamburgh, Castle Barnard, Dunstanburgh and Scarborough. Similarly, Carlisle was used as a supply-centre for the western defences, based on Skinburness in Cumberland and Caernarvon Castle in north Wales.[9] The sheriffs of the various counties were responsible for the collection and delivery of foodstuffs for the war. For example, the sheriff of Surrey and Sussex was ordered to organize the collection of large amounts of grain, salted meat and fish, which were then packed into barrels and sent by sea from Seaford and Shoreham, in Sussex, to Newcastle, but very little ever reached its destination. If we look at this effect countrywide, we see so many resources being swallowed up in a series of unsuccessful attempts to conquer Scotland.[10]

Having sent out the order for the muster, Edward then led his forces into Scotland once more. Among those who accompanied the army on this occasion was the King's illegitimate son, called Adam. The accounts for 1322 include payments for armour and other items of military equipment for Adam, who was openly described as 'the bastard son of the King'. He was probably a boy in his teens, since he was in the care of a tutor *(magister)*, named Hugh Chastilloun. If he had been born during 1307, following the banishment of Gavaston, he would have been about 15 years old at this time. It is noteworthy that Edward himself had been 16 years old when he first joined his father on an expedition to Scotland. Apart from six payments for armour for him in the financial records, there seem to be no other references to the boy.[11] The King was also concerned for the safety of his wife. He sent orders to the constable of Norham Castle, not far from Berwick, telling him to be watchful and saying that he had sent the Queen to Tynemouth for protection, while he himself was going through Northumberland, collecting a force as he went. The Scots, however, knowing that the army was coming, disappeared into the hills, taking all the corn and cattle with them. Frustratingly, Edward found no resistance to his advance, but he found no supplies either, and he was forced to withdraw. Again he received petitions from those who lived in the Borders, telling him of their continued sufferings during the past eight years. They declared they now had nothing left and it was useless for him to appoint wardens to keep the peace. They wanted nothing less than the King to advance, leading a full-scale army to crush the Scots.[12]

A chronicler provides a graphic description of the English soldiers returning home, desperate for food, dying because they gorged themselves when they found something to eat and so their stomachs burst. The campaign was admittedly a failure and the King was almost captured by Bruce in an encounter near Rievaulx Abbey in Yorkshire, as he made his way south. The Scots were catching up with him but, by riding very fast, 'fearful and unarmed', he managed to escape and to reach York in safety. The Scots, flushed with their successes, captured John, Earl of Richmond, and returned home laden with loot. Edward spent Christmas at York where, according to a chronicler, he ignored 'the shameful losses, which he had recently received among the Scots, and showed a joyful expression, although his heart was savagely tormented'.[13] In spite of the privations suffered by the army, there was no lack of provisions for the Household, as the clerk of the kitchens organized supplies of beef, mutton, pork, wild boar, veal, venison, rabbits, bream, salmon, pike, lampreys, eels, porpoise, sturgeon, crabs, swans, peacocks, capons, herons and pigeons. The King provided his wife with a gift of 20 pieces of sturgeon, while he sent 13 pieces of the same to Eleanor Despenser and 11 pike to the Dominicans at Langley. Other close friends of the King received gifts of deer and venison.[14] During the campaign the King was surrounded by his personal guard of five Gascon crossbowmen and 42 archers, while a large company of carpenters, sawyers and plasterers were employed over the year to attend to work on his private apartments.[15] The upkeep of such an establishment at York put great stress on the economy of the northern counties, which were expected to provide necessities for the King. Just one item, such as the supply of fodder for his horses, was a heavy drain on the surrounding countryside. In addition, the war left the King heavily in debt. His main creditor was Despenser the younger, while he owed his half-brother, the Earl of Norfolk large sums of money, 'for his expenses in the Scottish wars.'[16]

One writer blamed Despenser for the failure of the expedition, quoting it as yet another example of the King being misled by his bad advice.[17] In the event, the King left Yorkshire and had returned to London by April, leaving the officials of the Exchequer to follow slightly later. In the meantime, the Queen went on pilgrimages to visit various shrines throughout the country.[18] A chronicler painted a dismal picture of the year that was:

destructive, shameful, and lamentable for England because of struggles within the kingdom and the murder of the nobles; it was particularly disgraceful for the King because of his tyrannical behaviour towards his own people. He was hated for his failures in the North and in Scotland, where he destroyed almost half his people by his witless behaviour.[19]

In fact, during 1322, the overall economic situation had improved to some extent, while the short truce with the Scots had helped to ease the burdens of taxation. Nevertheless, the situation in the north remained desperate. The *Memoranda Rolls* recorded, 'great peril from the raids of the Scots who were ravaging and totally destroying' lands in Yorkshire.[20] There was so much suffering that Andrew Harclay, now rewarded with the title of Earl of Carlisle because he had brought victory to the King at Boroughbridge, suggested that England and Scotland should be separate and equal kingdoms. By negotiating with Bruce and by removing Edward's claims to overlordship, Harclay had hoped to bring some kind of peace to the troubled Borders. However, when news of his plan reached the King, the Earl was arrested and executed as a traitor. He had proposed setting up a council, composed of six Englishmen and six Scotsmen, which would settle disputes that affected both kingdoms. The significance of his proposal lay in its attempt to form a council that was independent of the King. Harclay's solution was, in effect, an open statement of the King's incapacity, or unwillingness, to deal with the problems of the Border country. Having removed Harclay, Edward replaced him with Edmund, Earl of Kent, who was appointed to take charge of the Border regions.[21]

Eventually, by the summer of 1323, a truce was drawn up between the English and the Scots, intended to last for 13 years, which allowed some kind of peace to return to the Border country. Effectively, it acknowledged the independence of Scotland and the inability of the English to impose any form of overlordship. On the face of it, the truce should have allowed the King to live in peace; he had successfully suppressed the rebels in England and Wales; he had the company of his dear friends, the Despensers, and Parliament was compliant with his wishes. However, such tranquillity was short-lived. The truce with Scotland brought only temporary relief, as war began to threaten in Gascony. The French King, Charles IV, who had recently succeeded his brother, Philip, was building a *bastide* (a fortified town) to protect the Benedictine priory of St Sardos in the district of Guienne. Although St Sardos had been granted to Edward I in 1279 as part of his possessions in Gascony, the Abbot of St Sardos claimed to be under the protection of the French King and, at the Abbot's request, Charles IV gave the order for the *bastide* to be built. Work began in October 1323, but it stopped when a group of armed men from Gascony raided the site and burned it. Charles IV reacted by declaring that Gascony and the county of Ponthieu were under French control. Edward contemplated an invasion of Gascony but he avoided open confrontation and sent the Bishops of Norwich and Winchester as envoys to the French court to negotiate a settlement.[22]

XXIV   OPPOSITION IN ENGLAND

Although the King had defeated the Contrariants at Boroughbridge, another party of opposition to the King and the Despensers began to emerge. The leaders of this group were the Queen and two churchmen, Adam Orleton, Bishop of Hereford, and Henry Burghersh, Bishop of Lincoln. Both men had supported the rebels in 1322 and the Bishop of Hereford, in particular, had links with Roger Mortimer. He had supposedly helped Mortimer to get out of the Tower in a well-planned escape. The story goes that, with the Queen's help, the guards at the Tower were drugged and so Mortimer was able to make his way into the kitchen of the royal apartments, from where he climbed up inside the chimney and escaped on to the roof. Using a rope-ladder, he let himself down the outside of the building into a rowing-boat which conveyed him across the Thames. Horses were ready for him on the other bank and he made his way to the Isle of Wight, where a ship was moored, ready to take him to Normandy. He landed on the coast of Normandy and made his way to Paris. The large number of writs issued for his arrest is a clear sign of the unease felt by the King and his supporters at his escape. They seem to have assumed that Mortimer would go to France and then establish himself in Ireland, where he had been appointed governor in 1316. However, he stayed in France.[1]

There were increasing indications of further opposition to the King. In January 1323, a group of men, who had supported the rebels, decided to show their resentment at the continued and unjust imprisonment of the Contrariants. They made a plan to attack the Tower of London and the castles at Winsdor and Wallingford, to release the prisoners kept there. They began by launching an assault upon Wallingford Castle, where Maurice Berkeley and Hugh Audley were held. They entered secretly by the postern gate from the River Thames, but were then discovered. The local people were alerted by the noise and besieged the attackers until the Earl of Kent and Despenser the elder arrived with a force of armed men. The original attackers could not withstand this violent onslaught and took refuge in the chapel within the castle. In spite of appeals by the clergy, they were dragged out and either put to death straightaway or imprisoned until the King decided how to punish them. Fear of similar attacks on other strongholds used as prisons caused the King to strengthen his castles and to move prisoners from place to place, keeping them under stricter supervision. At Windsor, for example, rebuilding work included fitting new locks and iron bars to the entrances of the White Tower and other towers, 'to hold the prisoners there'.[2]

Beginning in September 1323, the King travelled through northern England, through County Durham, Lancashire and Yorkshire, holding enquiries concerning law and order, punishing wrongdoers and enforcing the law. He was travelling through the lands that were once held by Thomas of Lancaster and were now in the possession of the Crown. But most of them were virtually worthless, having suffered continual devastation by both English and Scottish armies. The King was forced to act, as the cases of recorded crimes across these northern counties increased dramatically, giving rise to a situation in which local organizations were inadequate to deal with the degree of unrest.[3] Edward briefly abandoned his task to celebrate Christmas in magnificent style at Kenilworth Castle, which was formerly Lancaster's. From time to time, the castle had been under royal control and, during the reign of King John, it had been one of the largest castles in the country. Henry III had granted it to his brother, the Earl of Lancaster, and so it had passed to Thomas of Lancaster, but it was now, once more, in the hands of the King. Leaving Kenilworth, Edward travelled westwards to Despenser's castle at Hanley and then south to Berkeley Castle in Gloucestershire, again enforcing the law throughout the lands of the Contrariants. He visited the towns and cities of the Welsh Marches, making rigorous enquiries and ruthlessly suppressing any ringleaders who were identified as troublemakers. The general lawlessness, devastation and poverty had forced many to live as outlaws and robbers and these, too, were savagely punished. Following the suppression of the Contrariants, who had been responsible for the management of these lands, large areas of the country had become ungoverned and ungovernable. It was a society on the verge of collapse and the King was left to intervene personally to deal with a high level of disorder that had resulted from the breakup of the social fabric.[4] Under such a regime, it was not surprising that support for the Queen began to grow. The Bishops of Hereford and Lincoln were joined by John Stratford, Bishop of Winchester. Another supporter was Henry of Lancaster, who had succeeded his brother Thomas. In addition, the King's two half-brothers, Thomas, Earl of Norfolk, and Edmund, Earl of Kent, voiced their criticism of the King. Even Henry Beaumont, Edward's boyhood friend, who was formerly a member of the King's council, now withdrew his support. In reply to this increasingly vocal opposition, the Despensers turned to attack the Queen, whom they saw as the source of trouble. A chronicler wrote of the younger Despenser who,

> When he saw the Queen's displeasure, by his subtle wit, he set great discord between the King and Queen, so that the King would not see the Queen nor come in her company.[5]

There were even rumours that Despenser was applying to the papal court to get the royal marriage annulled. He further antagonized her by ordering the confiscation of her estates. He claimed that this was done for security reasons, on the grounds that the French were about to invade and might use her estates as a base after they had landed. Isabella was given an annual allowance in compensation, which was reasonably generous, but the change meant that she lost control of her property, particularly her dower rights.[6] In fury and despair, Isabella wrote letters to her brother Charles IV, King of France, declaring that she was treated with no more consideration than a servant in her husband's palace. She also went on to complain about the loss of her French servants, since there were orders to arrest all French people in England.[7]

Edward was back in London by February 1324. A meeting of Parliament was held at which there was a discussion concerning the request from the French King that Edward should go to France to perform homage for Gascony and other English lands in France. The decision was made that the King should not go to France, but should send envoys to ask for a postponement. At the same meeting, the Bishop of Hereford was charged with treason, on the grounds that he had supported the enemies of the King by helping Mortimer to escape from the Tower. The Bishop denied the charges and declared that he was answerable only to the Archbishop of Canterbury, the Pope and his fellow Bishops. They should decide his fate, not the King. The clergy who were present begged the King to show mercy. However, he refused to listen to their pleas and handed the Bishop over to the custody of the Archbishop, before deciding what further measures to take against him. The uproar that followed among the clergy led the King to take further action. He summoned his Justices who declared that the Bishop of Hereford was guilty; his lands and property were confiscated and he was kept in the custody of the Archbishop. In contrast, the Bishop of Lincoln, whose possessions had been held by the King for two years, had them restored. In cases like this, the sheer unpredictability of the King's actions generated fear and confusion among many.[8]

There was a further sign of open opposition to the King in March 1324 when Parliament presented a formal plea that the bodies of those who had been hanged after the battle of Boroughbridge might be taken down and decently buried. The rotting corpses must have presented a grisly reminder two years after the battle. The King complied with the wishes of Parliament and issued orders to the sheriffs:

> to permit the bodies of the late rebels still hanging on gibbets to be taken down by those who wish, to be buried in the churchyards of the parish churches nearest to where the rebels were hanged and not elsewhere.[9]

XXV   ISABELLA IN FRANCE

The English envoys, who had been sent to France to negotiate a settlement following the destruction of the *bastide* at St Sardos, had failed to make any progress and their lack of success gave Isabella an excuse to visit France. The Pope's ambassadors acknowledged her skills and proposed that she should go to Paris, in an attempt to negotiate an agreement between her brother and her husband. Edward reluctantly agreed to allow her to go. The French chronicler, Froissart, depicts her making a dramatic, secret journey, pretending that she was going on a pilgrimage to Canterbury, from where she travelled to Winchelsea and then took ship to France. However, the secret nature of her journey seems unlikely, since she was accompanied by a large retinue, including her huntsman and a pack of hounds, which were left behind at Canterbury, to be maintained at the expense of the unfortunate Prior.[1] The Queen, accompanied by the Earl of Kent, reached Boulogne, where she stayed for two days. From there, she went to Paris, where she was warmly welcomed by her brother, whom she had not seen for many years. She recounted to him all her problems with the Despensers and he responded favourably by offering her financial support. Isabella was also successful in completing her mission to settle the dispute between England and France. She negotiated an agreement in which Edward's French lands would be restored to him when he performed homage for them in person. Until that time, Gascony would be managed by a French governor.

In meetings at Dover and Wingham (Kent) Archbishop Reynolds and several Bishops followed up the agreement negotiated by Isabella and suggested that Edward should go to France in person to do homage, as the Pope's envoys had advised. Extensive preparations were made for the journey, Prince Edward was appointed as Keeper of the realm during the King's absence, while the northern counties were placed under the control of Anthony Lucy and the Earl of Arundel was given command of the Welsh Marches.[2] But the Despensers, who feared for their safety if the King went to France without them, wished to keep him away from the influence of Isabella and they advised him to send Prince Edward to do homage on his behalf. The King accepted their advice and claimed that he was not well enough to make the journey to France. As a result, at Dover in 1325, Prince Edward, at the age of 13, was formally invested with the counties of Ponthieu and Montreuil and the Duchy of Gascony. On September 12th 1325 he sailed to France, accompanied by the Bishops of Exeter and Winchester and Henry Beaumont.[3] In the presence of many French noblemen, he performed homage to his uncle, the King of France, at the royal hunting-lodge at Vincennes, just outside Paris. Lavish gifts were exchanged and the Prince made a good impression on the French.

There is no direct evidence that the King was unwell as he travelled through the south-east of England, instead of going to France. He stayed at Guildford Castle, in Surrey, where his officials had recently spent £90 on repairing the 'King's houses within the castle' and 'the paling of the King's park and the lodge within it'.[4] He also stayed at Bletchingley, in Surrey, on the estate which had once been part of the Clare inheritance and then passed to Audley through his marriage to Margaret Gavaston. Here, too, work was carried out hurriedly to make it ready for him: the living quarters and the chapel apartments were provided with new roofs 'for the arrival of the King'. Edward probably enjoyed hunting in the extensive parks there, which included a heronry.[5] From Bletchingley, he went to East Grinstead, in Sussex, and then returned to Surrey, staying at Banstead in the manor-house which had been granted to Isabella in 1318.[6] After a brief visit to Westminster, he stayed for several days at Sheen, in Surrey, which had recently become a Chamber manor. As at Bletchingley, building alterations were carried out prior to his visit.[7]

By the end of September, after Prince Edward had performed homage to the King of France, Edward was expecting his wife and his son to return to England. But the Queen and the Prince, having sent back the greater part of their retinues, remained in France. Some said that they were kept there against their wishes, while others reported that they had deliberately stayed away because the Queen had fallen in love with Roger Mortimer. There were rumours that she would not return unless she could bring Mortimer with her. The Bishop of Exeter was closely involved in the diplomatic assignment and, as Treasurer, was responsible for the expenses of the visit. When he became aware of the suspicions surrounding the Queen's motives, he fled from her court, fearing that he might be murdered. He was so fearful that he abandoned his household in France and returned secretly to England. Some said that he disguised himself as a merchant; others believed that he was dressed as a pilgrim. He reached England by September 29th and immediately alerted the King and his friends to his suspicions concerning the Queen's intentions. During this time, the King was staying at Portchester Castle on the south coast, where he had organized a major programme of rebuilding to strengthen and extend the castle.[8] He appointed commissioners who were responsible for protecting the coastline against a possible invasion by the French and, yet again, he ordered all the French people in England to be arrested. At the same time, he wrote to Isabella, strongly urging her to return, but she stated her opinions quite clearly in her letters to her husband. She declared that she knew that there had been attempts to destroy her marriage and she would not return until the person responsible had been removed. In the meantime, she considered herself to be a widow. Her brother, the French King, was willing to let her stay in France for as long as she wished or to supply her with money to pay for an army to invade England.

Edward replied to her arguments with a defence of the Despensers, saying that her fears were imaginary and that she had been misled by 'some unknown, evil enemy', referring to Mortimer. On December 1st, Edward wrote to the French King, expressing his concern at the Queen's absence and warning him about 'English traitors at the French court'. He also wrote to Isabella, making it clear that she had no reason to be afraid of the Despensers:

> If either Hugh or any other living being in our dominions would wish to do her ill, and it came to our knowledge, we would chastise him in a manner that should be an example to all others; and this is, and always will be, our entire will.

Edward went on to say that she had shown no obvious signs of hostility to the Despensers before she left for France and, in fact, had behaved quite amicably towards them, showing them 'tokens of the firmest friendship'.

Edward then wrote to his son the following day, urging him to return without his mother, if she insisted on staying in France. The King again wrote to his son in March the following year from Lichfield, in Staffordshire. Edward's letter betrays his anxieties for the future. He begged his son to return without the Queen and he especially urged him not to enter a marriage contract without his father's consent. He went on to declare once more that Isabella had nothing to fear from Despenser the younger, 'who, has always and so well loyally served us'. He then referred to the Queen's relationship with Mortimer:

> She openly, notoriously, and knowing it to be contrary to her duty, and against the welfare of our Crown, has attracted to herself, and retains in her company, the Mortimer, our traitor and mortal foe, proved, attainted and adjudged; and him she accompanies in the house and abroad in despite of us, of our Crown, and the right ordering of our realm.

The King emphasized that, by associating with such a villain as Mortimer, the Prince was bringing shame and dishonour upon himself.[9] The reference to a marriage contract for the Prince shows that the King had been informed about Isabella's intention to arrange an alliance for her son, without the consent of the King and Parliament. Before the Queen and the Prince had left for France, Edward had been negotiating a marriage between the Prince and Eleanor, Princess of Aragon. In fact, he had already asked the Pope to grant a dispensation for the marriage, because of the close relationship between the two families.[10] In spite of these arrangements, Isabella went ahead with her own scheme and the Prince was betrothed to Philippa, daughter of William, Count of Hainault, who also ruled Holland and Zeeland. The bride's dowry was paid in advance and Isabella was able to use this money to support herself and her friends while they remained in France.

Edward was now faced with the prospect of a joint invasion by the Queen of England and the King of France, aided by the Hainaulters. Her leading supporters, the Earls of Kent and Richmond, the Bishop of Winchester, Henry Beaumont and Roger Mortimer, gathered around her in Paris, while many others also flocked to join her party. At the threat of this combined attack, the King once more reviewed the state of his castles. Assessments were made of the armaments, weaknesses and available supplies across southern England: at Dover, Leeds, London, Odiham, Tonbridge, Wallingford and Windsor. Similar reviews were made in north Wales: at Beaumaris, Caernarvon, Conwy and Harlech. Scarborough Castle was established as the main focus of Edward's defence in northern England. The assessors listed the equipment at each castle and sent requests for carpenters and workmen to maintain the fortifications and the siege-engines.[11] At the Tower of London, the wall facing the Thames was strengthened and four of the towers were repaired. Purchases for the Tower included 500 lbs of hair from horses' manes and the tails of cows and oxen, 'for making cords for the King's springalds and other engines'.[12] Parliament was summoned in October and met at the Tower of London on November 18th, but very little was decided because people were afraid to criticize the King. The session was transferred to Westminster and was then dissolved on November 29th, having achieved nothing. On that day, when the Bishop of Rochester left London and was travelling through Kent, he met members of the Queen's entourage returning from France. They claimed that the Bishop of Exeter had fled from France without paying their expenses. The resultant shortage of money had forced Isabella to send them back to England, while she remained in France.[13]

Isabella's obvious success in gaining support abroad stirred both her husband and the Despensers to action. Edward's letter to the French King, also written from Lichfield, shows the extent of accusations and counter-accusations. Isabella had declared that she had concealed her hatred for the Despensers and had pretended to show them friendship, because she feared what actions they might take against her. In his reply, Edward accused her of lying, saying that she had gone to France to make peace, but had lied to her brother about the treatment she had received at home. The King put the blame squarely on her 'disordered will' and her passion for Mortimer. He then urged her brother, Charles, to punish her for her outrageous behaviour and to ignore 'the passing whim of a woman'. He also expressed his concern for Prince Edward, fearing that he was being wrongly influenced by his mother and Mortimer, 'that traitor and enemy'. The Pope, at the instigation of Edward and the Despensers, was also making similar requests to Charles, urging him to abandon support for Isabella and Mortimer. In a further letter to his son, the King referred to his fears about the bad influence of Mortimer, noting that Mortimer had publicly accompanied him in the coronation procession of the Queen of France. Edward saw this as a great dishonour to the English throne, describing Mortimer as 'neither a suitable companion for your mother, nor for you, and we hold that much evil to the country will come of it'. The King pleaded with his son to comply with his wishes, pointing out that a dutiful son should obey his father, lest 'all other sons will take example to be disobedient to their lords and fathers'.[14]

Edward persuaded all the Bishops to write to the Queen, pleading with her to return. They did as the King requested and wrote to her, expressing their fears that her refusal to return and her hostility to just one person (Despenser) would bring about war with France and general devastation in England.[15] However, their pleas had no effect and she refused to return. As a result, both she and the Prince were branded as public enemies and they, and all their supporters, were banished from the kingdom.[16] In desperation, the Despensers used their money and influence to try to turn more people against Isabella by stressing the rumours about her relationship with Mortimer. They were clearly successful in persuading the French King and some of his ministers to withdraw their support for her:

> They sent secret messengers to France with plenty of gold and silver and rich jewels, and especially to the King and his Privy Council. They did so much that, in a short space, the King of France and all his Privy Council were as cold to help the Queen in her voyage as they had before great desire to do it.[17]

Charles reacted by refusing to support his sister any more and he banned all Frenchmen from helping her. Similar bribes by the Despensers to eminent church leaders and other clergy close to the Pope kept up the pressure on the Pope to continue making his protests to Charles, condemning the Queen.

XXVI INVASION

During the spring and summer of 1326 Edward was energetically organizing the defence of England. On August 12th, he summoned the fleet to assemble at Portsmouth, 'to repel the French'. A few days later, he ordered a watch to be kept along the east coast, northwards from the Thames estuary, and again he issued orders for the arrest of all French people in England. At the beginning of September he was at Portchester once more, where he commanded all French monks living near the coast to be moved to monasteries further inland, in case they aided the invaders. He also put leading men in command of vulnerable areas of the country. For example, he still trusted his half-brother, the Earl of Norfolk, and made him responsible for the defence of East Anglia, while he put the Bishop of Exeter in charge of Devon and Cornwall. Furthermore, he attempted to protect northern England by commanding the Bishop of Durham to fortify the castles at Dunstanburgh, Norham and York against the Scots. He complained about the neglect of the defences at Dover Castle and ordered further armaments for the Tower of London.[1] In September the King took further action. He launched an attack on Normandy, perhaps with the aim of rescuing Prince Edward. The invasion failed and the fleet of at least 130 ships was driven back.[2]

There were even rumours that the King was planning to have his wife and son murdered.[3] But for his part, Edward steadfastly maintained that he wanted his wife to return to him, declaring that it was not his fault that she had left and that he still loved her and wanted his marriage to continue. All these pleas eventually persuaded Charles to banish his sister, ordering her to return to England with her son. Froissart depicts the situation at the French court, where the French nobles were threatened with banishment and loss of their lands if they attempted to communicate with Isabella. Her only support came from Robert of Artois, Count of Beaumont, who helped her in secret. When he discovered that the French King was planning to use force to send the Queen, Prince Edward and the Earl of Kent back to England, Artois advised her to flee at once to Hainault and place herself under the protection of the Count of Hainault. She listened to his advice and, taking her friends with her, she found refuge and support in Hainault.

In addition, the betrothal of Prince Edward to Philippa of Hainault was formalized.

With the help of the Hainaulters, the Queen was able to muster an army. Count William supplied a fleet which gathered in the ports of Holland and Zeeland, while his brother, John of Hainault, provided a force of armed men. Isabella set sail with a considerable army from Dordrecht in Holland on September 23rd 1326. The King had called the English fleet to assemble, but the sailors declared that they were unwilling to fight for him, on the grounds that the younger Despenser had caused such trouble across the English seas during his time of exile.[4] Robert Wateville was in charge of the King's fleet that was operating off the east coast but he, too, refused to support the King. He had changed sides twice over the years, first rebelling against the King, then entering the service of the younger Despenser. In 1326, he changed sides once more and gave his allegiance to the Queen.[5] She landed unopposed at Orwell, in Suffolk, on the Earl of Norfolk's estates, where she was certain of good reception. She then reached Harwich, in Essex, where people flocked to join her cause. Norfolk himself was there to welcome her and he was joined by Henry of Lancaster, with numerous noblemen, knights and church leaders. Others, notably Walter Reynolds, Archbishop of Canterbury, provided her with money. The Queen's army moved to Bury St Edmunds and then to Cambridge, where she stayed at Barnwell Priory. From Barnwell, she went to Baldock, in Hertfordshire, where her forces encountered Thomas Baldock, the brother of Robert Baldock, the King's Chancellor. They captured him and ransacked his property. *The Annals of St Paul's* declared that only the goods of the King's supporters, such as the Baldocks and the Despensers, were plundered, while the possessions of others were left unscathed. As Isabella journeyed across the country she gathered further support and found no opposition.[6]

The King was staying in the Tower of London at the time of the landing. At first he refused to believe the news, thinking that it must be a rumour. But when confirmation arrived, he ordered the sheriffs of the eastern counties to call out over 50,000 men to support him. Although he was not bound to pay their wages, since they would be fighting for the defence of the realm, he told the sheriffs to make payments in the meantime and claim recompence later. He also requested help from the citizens of London, who held a meeting and made known their decision, which was a masterpiece of evasion. They promised to help the King, the Queen and the Prince, since the kingdom was rightfully theirs, but they would close the gates to traitors. They were unwilling to leave London to go out and fight unless they could return before sunset. This limited support forced the King to take action. He left his younger son, John of

Eltham, at the Tower, in the care of Eleanor, wife of Despenser the younger, and issued a proclamation that all should resist and kill the invaders, with the exception of the Queen, the Prince, and the Earl of Kent, who should be taken unharmed.[7]

Edward ordered a papal bull against invaders, which had been used in earlier years against the Scots, to be read out in St Paul's Cathedral and in other churches, but it failed to gain him any support. In London, it served only to rouse feelings against him.[8] He also offered a reward of £1000 for the body of Roger Mortimer, alive or dead. In his anxiety to intercept spies, he appointed Richard Fille, a skilled sailor, whom he had used on earlier missions, to be Keeper of the River Thames. Fille was ordered to arrest any people whom he suspected of carrying secret messages into or out of the country and to search their ships. The King then set off westwards in the company of the two Despensers, Robert Baldock, and Simon of Reading, who was commanded to bring 100 infantrymen from Oxfordshire and Berkshire. As he went, the King sent orders to the sheriffs of the western counties to call out men to support him. He particularly ordered supplies for Berkeley Castle, which was to be equipped with a full complement of fighting men. In a desperate attempt to increase the size of his army, the King ordered a proclamation to be made, 'at least two or three times a week, at (county) courts, fairs, markets and other places', saying that he would pardon, 'felons, outlaws or former supporters of his enemies', if they joined him.[9]

The Queen, in turn, issued her own proclamation, declaring that all should hope for the benefits of peace, except for the Despensers and Baldock and their supporters, because these men were responsible for the troubled state of the country. She went further and promised that anyone who brought her the head of the younger Despenser would receive the sum of £2000 as a reward. Isabella also made an appeal to the citizens of London, asking for their help. In contrast to the evasive reply they had given to the King, they responded favourably to her and offered their undying support. As proof of their allegiance, they beheaded John Marshall, a Londoner, who had been secretary to the younger Despenser, accusing him of betraying the plans of the citizens to his master. They went on to plunder the house of the Bishop of Exeter, who had gone to France with Isabella but then returned to support the King. According to *The French Chronicle of London*, Edward had appointed the Bishop to be guardian of the city of London and to be responsible for its security. When the Bishop of Exeter discovered that the Londoners were supporting the Queen, he summoned the Mayor and demanded the keys of the gates from him. The Bishop's arrogance so annoyed the Londoners that, when he tried to cross the city and reach the safety of the Tower, he was forced to seek refuge in St Paul's. But they followed him and caught him at the north door of the cathedral. They struck him down and beheaded him and three of his men at Cheapside. The next day they murdered his treasurer. This was a signal for a general rising in London. The citizens looted and plundered the houses of any who might be associated with the King, including the houses of Robert Baldock and of the Italian bankers who had lent him money. They went to the Tower and set free the prisoners, demanding that Prince John, then aged ten, and the children of Roger Mortimer should be handed over to them. They claimed to be acting in support of the Prince and named him guardian of London and the Tower. On October 17th, the tablet which had commemorated the Ordinances was replaced in St Paul's. (It had been removed on the orders of the King after the Ordinances had been repealed).[10] The Archbishop of Canterbury was so terrified at the uprising and the murder of the Bishop of Exeter that he fled, riding 20 miles in an evening and even further the next day,

'We were so stunned at the terrible deed' he wrote to the Prior of Christchurch, Canterbury, 'that we left Lambeth and went to Croydon and even as far as Otford that same night, and on next day to Maidstone, where we are remaining.'[11]

London remained in a ferment until November 15th, when the Bishop of Winchester brought letters from the Queen, authorizing the election of a new Mayor. Richard of Bettoyne was elected; he was a supporter of Mortimer and a man who hated the Despensers. London was now secure for the Queen. She praised the devotion of the former Mayor and thanked him 'for his late bloody act, which was styled an excellent piece of justice'.[12]

The two sides in the conflict kept their distance; as the King was fleeing with just a few supporters, the Queen followed him with a much larger force. The King, accompanied by the Despensers and Baldock, was in Gloucester on October 10th and from there he went to Chepstow on the River Wye. While he was staying at Chepstow Castle, he placed the elder Despenser, who was then at Bristol, in charge of all the forces in the south-western counties, ranging from Hampshire to Cornwall, then Edward took refuge on board a ship in the Bristol Channel, with the younger Despenser, Baldock and a few others. The Queen went from London to Wallingford and then on to Oxford, where the Bishop of Hereford preached a sermon about rooting out evil government from the kingdom. Every day, the Queen's army increased in size and she was joined by Henry Percy and Thomas Wake, together with other forces from northern England.[13] She too travelled westwards, reaching Gloucester and then Berkeley Castle. She restored the castle and its surrounding estates, which extended across the county from Wotton to Slimbridge, to Thomas Berkeley. Thomas had been imprisoned in Wallingford Castle and deprived of his inheritance after his father had held out against the King. The Queen similarly restored lands to many others whose estates had been confiscated by the King.

Isabella then reached Bristol, which was held for the King by the elder Despenser. Her army laid siege to both the city and the castle. But, as with London, the citizens supported the Queen. Despenser was forced to surrender without any resistance. He was brought before a commission at Bristol headed by William Trussell of Lancaster. Trussell had supported Thomas of Lancaster and, having fought against the King at Boroughbridge, he had escaped abroad and then returned with Isabella. He was joined on the commission by Henry of Lancaster, the Earls of Kent and Norfolk, Roger Mortimer, Thomas Wake and other leading men. They charged Despenser with treachery, with taking royal powers, and with advising the King to do harm to his subjects. They further accused him of robbing the kingdom, inflicting cruelty on all and using his influence to damage the power of the Church. They sentenced him to be hanged, drawn and beheaded, with his head to be sent to Winchester, which was the seat of his earldom. As a final disgrace, because his life had been so dishonourable, they ordered him to be hung in a surcoat (over-garment) bearing his own coat-of-arms.[14]

The King was still trying to evade his captors by sailing along the River Severn and into the Bristol Channel, perhaps hoping to reach Lundy Island and escape from there to Ireland. Marlowe portrays Despenser urging the King to make for Ireland:

Fly, fly my Lord; the Queen is overstrong.
Shape we our course to Ireland, there to breathe.[15]

But Ireland was beyond their reach and they eventually landed on the coast of south Wales, in Glamorgan. Even the massive stronghold of Caerphilly Castle could not provide a refuge and Despenser was forced to surrender it to the Queen. The King moved further west, going as far as Neath, where he used both the abbey and the castle to accommodate his retinue which included Baldock, Despenser and Simon of Reading. They stayed at Neath for about a week while Edward continued to issue royal commands, authenticated by the Great Seal.[16] The King had taken with him a large number of possessions, including gold and silver plate, a great deal of armour and four beds, together with large sums of money which he hoped to use to raise an army. On November 5th he was still issuing orders to raise troops from Gower and he followed these with instructions for supplies to be brought from Swansea Castle for his supposed army in Gower. However, there was no response to any of his commands and, by November 10th, he was forced to open negotiations with Isabella. The details of the next few days are uncertain but the general outline is clear. The Queen and Roger Mortimer were at Hereford, from where they sent Henry of Lancaster, with an armed force, to find both Edward and Despenser the younger. The King fled once more, leaving behind much of his wealth and many of his possessions at Neath and Swansea. He may have been trying to make for Ireland but gave up the attempt and moved eastwards, perhaps hoping to regain Caerphilly Castle. However, he failed to reach Caerphilly and was probably caught close to Llantrisant Castle, which belonged to the Despensers. Local tradition has recorded the place of his capture as Pantybrad (Vale of Treachery).[17]

On November 16th, Lancaster brought him to the town of Monmouth, where he surrendered the Great Seal to the Bishop of Hereford. The seal was then delivered to Isabella and Prince Edward at Much Marcle, not far from Hereford.[18] From Monmouth, the King was taken to Kenilworth Castle, where he had celebrated a magnificent Christmas feast just a few years before. The three other prisoners, Despenser, Baldock and Simon of Reading were brought to the Queen at Hereford and she gave the promised reward of £2000 to the captors. Some of the other supporters of the King, including the Earl of Arundel, were beheaded by Mortimer. The younger Despenser, like his father, was brought before a commission, consisting of William Trussel, Henry of Lancaster, the Earls of Kent and Norfolk, Mortimer and other leaders.[19] They held a so-called trial in Hereford, accusing him of countless crimes committed against the people, both in secret and in public. He made no answer to the charges and he was sentenced to death. Again like his father, he was hanged, drawn and quartered. However, his head was sent, not to Winchester, but to London, where it was placed on London Bridge. The other parts of his quartered body were sent to distant parts of the country. According to the French chronicler, Froissart, his genitals were cut off and burned before he died, as a symbol of his 'heretical' behaviour. Although Froissart's versions of events are not particularly accurate, he may be reflecting the popular opinion that Despenser had a homosexual relationship with the King. The Bishop of Winchester, on behalf of the Queen, recovered some of the Despensers' treasure, worth many pounds, which had been left at the Tower of London, while their lands and estates across the country were plundered and devastated. As a typical example, the estates of the younger Despenser that lay to the south of London were ransacked. A wide area of land in Surrey, stretching from Bagshot, Pirbright, Woking and Leatherhead as far as Vauxhall and Kennington, was laid waste. The only exception was Tolworth, a large moated manor-house near Kingston-upon-Thames, which was acquired by the Earl of Kent. Simon of Reading, who had fled with the King, was also executed. His body hung from the same gallows as Despenser but ten feet lower, since he was less important and his guilt was less. A chronicler recorded that these executions took place on a Monday, out of a desire to avenge the death of Thomas of Lancaster, which had occurred on a Monday. Baldock, Chancellor to the King and Canon of St Paul's, was also charged with committing crimes against the people but the Bishop of Hereford pleaded that his life should be spared because he was a clergyman. He was handed over to the Bishop who put him in prison. He was later taken to London and imprisoned at Newgate, where he died soon afterwards from ill-treatment at the hands of the Londoners who despised him.[20]

XXVII DEPOSITION

The King was arrested in November but, even before he was captured, the Queen had taken the initiative by issuing a proclamation at Bristol, announcing that Prince Edward was now Keeper of the realm. Even so, following the recovery of the Great Seal, the Queen and her advisers continued to issue documents in the name of the King, presenting the fiction that he was still in control. It is very likely that, once Isabella had achieved her aim of destroying the Despensers, she did not agitate for the King to be deposed; the demands for his deposition seem to have come largely from Mortimer and his supporters. Finally, at a meeting in Hereford, leading nobles and churchmen swore allegiance to the Prince, appointing the Bishop of Norwich as Chancellor and the Bishop of Hereford as Treasurer. From that moment, Edward II was effectively deposed. The Queen spent Christmas at Wallingford with her children and Mortimer.[1]

When Parliament met at Westminster in January, the official processes of deposition began. Those who had lost their lands to the King and the Despensers recovered their estates, while the citizens of London swore allegiance to the Queen and Prince Edward, declaring that their quarrel had been with the Despensers, not with members of the royal family. At about the same time, the nobles, with William Trussell as their spokesman *(procurator)*, renounced their homage to their former King. Leading churchmen also made their position clear. On January 13th 1327, the Bishop of Hereford took his text from the *Book of Ecclesiastes*, 'A foolish King shall ruin his people'. The next day, the Bishop of Winchester took his text from the *Book of Kings*, 'my head pains me', explaining what a feeble head England had. The following day, the Archbishop of Canterbury preached a sermon in Westminster Hall, declaring that the King had been deposed with the consent of all. He stated uncompromisingly, 'The voice of the people is the voice of God'.[2] By these means, the nobles and clergy presented the deposition as a formal and legal act. On the other hand, they had no legal precedent for deposition and Prince Edward, now aged 14, refused to accept the crown without the consent of his father. A deputation immediately set out for Kenilworth, where the King was kept under guard. The members of the delegation were deliberately chosen to represent all groups within the kingdom; it included clergymen, nobles and representatives from the counties, from London and other towns, cities and ports. The Articles of Deposition were drawn up, which formalized their complaints. They stated that Edward had been an incompetent ruler, had refused to listen to good advice, that he had destroyed the Church and had been responsible for the loss of Scotland, Ireland and Gascony. In addition to this, he had failed to act justly and had reduced his kingdom to poverty. He was weak and cruel, and had totally failed to change his behaviour in spite of so many protests.[3]

Two Bishops were already with the King, trying to persuade him to come to London, when the full deputation arrived at Kenilworth on January 20th 1327. The delegates told Edward that his son had been chosen to replace him and they earnestly begged him to give up the throne without opposition and allow his son to rule. At the same time, they promised him that he would be allowed to continue to live in a manner suitable to his rank. But behind their demands there was a distinct fear that some people might rebel and choose a person outside the royal family as ruler, possibly even Mortimer. Even if the King refused to abdicate, the delegates swore to perform homage to his son and to continue with the plans they had already made. The King, dressed in black, responded with tears and showed deep grief at their request. Finally, deciding that he had no alternative, he begged for pardon from all who had come and thanked them for choosing his eldest son as his successor. The delegates renounced their homage to him and, from that moment, his official Household ceased to exist. Messengers immediately returned to Parliament with the King's reply, bringing with them the regalia of orb, crown and sceptre. On January 24th, Edward III was named as the new King. He was crowned at Westminster on February 1st, 'chosen by the whole kingdom, and with the consent of his father'.[4] As a way of calming down the ferment in London, a general pardon was granted to all the citizens for any offences committed between the time of the Queen's landing and the Coronation. Pardons were also granted throughout the country as a means of bringing disputes to a conclusion. The long lists of pardons for murders and other offences, committed by supporters of both sides, are clear evidence for widespread unrest during the later years of the reign of Edward II. Furthermore, Edward's acknowledgement of his son as successor helped to smooth the path of revolution and, realistically, he had virtually no supporters, since the actions of the Despensers had antagonized any who might have helped him.[5]

Edward remained in relative comfort at Kenilworth in the care of Henry of Lancaster. But even a deposed King could still remain a threat to stability. While the detailed events of 1327 are difficult to interpret, the general outline can be made out. In April, Mortimer ordered Edward to be moved from Kenilworth to Berkeley Castle, where he could be more closely guarded. As soon as arrangements were made, he was transferred quickly, travelling 50 miles in two days, until the party reached Gloucester. From there, he was taken to Llanthony Abbey, where he spent the night as guest of the Augustinian Canons, and then travelled to Berkeley. The castle, built of red sandstone and grey stone, lies on a low hill, overlooking the estuary of the River Severn. It was a Norman castle, with a shell keep enclosing the central *motte*. The King was supposedly kept imprisoned in the tower known as the Thorpe Tower. The evidence for this period is elusive, but Marlowe's play offers the pitiful picture of the King's journey, which had appeared in the chronicles of John Stow, published in 1580, showing the degradation of a lonely King forced into a disguise as a poor man and having his beard shaved off with dirty water from a ditch. When he reached Berkeley he was placed in the care of Thomas Berkeley and John Maltravers. Thomas Berkeley had been previously imprisoned with his father, Maurice, and had lost his estates to the Despensers. However, Isabella had released him from prison and restored his lands to him. He had also married Mortimer's daughter, while Maltravers was married to Berkeley's sister. With this background of alliances, these keepers were likely to be loyal to the Queen and Mortimer, but they did not appear to ill-treat the King. They received an allowance of £5 a day from the Treasury, 'for the expenses of the household of the Lord Edward, sometime King of England', and the Berkeley household accounts contain references to ample supplies of wine, capons, eggs, cheese and beef, 'for the household of the King's father'.[6]

Eventually, two attempted rescues brought Edward's relative comfort to an end. The first occurred when a Dominican friar, called Thomas Dunhead, or Dunheved, organized a raid on Berkeley Castle. Some time earlier, Edward had apparently sent Dunhead as an envoy to the Pope to help him obtain a divorce from Isabella but, being unsuccessful in his petition, he returned to England. When he discovered that the King was in prison, he formed a conspiracy to organize an attack on Berkeley Castle. The details of his actions are not clear; we know only that Thomas Berkeley was ordered to arrest Dunhead and others 'because they had come to plunder the castle and refused to go on an expedition against the Scots'. This evidence suggests that there may have been some attempt to set Edward free, but there is no indication that the King was actually released. On the other hand, chroniclers provide vivid, perhaps fictitious, accounts of the King being rescued and taken to Corfe Castle, in Dorset, and to 'various other secret places'. According to them, he was finally recaptured and taken back to Berkeley. They paint a grim picture of the

King as a man in total confusion who scarcely knew where he was; this man, who had once been so strong and healthy, was now worn out by lack of sleep, constant travel and poor food. They also describe the actions of his keepers who tormented him by their treatment. Each one had charge of the King for a month at a time and they deliberately kept him a state of suspense by alternating their attitude; Berkeley treated him kindly, while Maltravers was harsh and cruel. In the meantime, the Queen apparently sent her husband fine clothes and soothing letters, but refused to see him, on the grounds that the leading men of the country would not allow it.[7]

XXVIII   DEATH OF A KING

The second plot to free the King was hatched in Wales by Rhys ap Griffith, possibly out of hostility to Mortimer rather than any concern for Edward. In September, Mortimer received news of the conspiracy and feared that there might be a successful rescue. He immediately sent one of his men, William Ogle, or Ockley, from Abergavenny in Monmouthshire, to Berkeley Castle, with a message for Maltravers and Thomas Gurney, who was then acting as Thomas Berkeley's deputy. The message was supposedly written in Latin by the Bishop of Hereford, stating *'Edwardum occidere nolite timere bonum est'*. This could be translated in two ways: 'Do not be afraid to kill Edward, it is a good thing,' or 'Do not kill Edward, it is good to be afraid'. Within two weeks, the King was dead.[1] There were many rumours about his death; fourteenth-century chronicles referred to him being 'foully murdered' at Berkeley without receiving the sacrament. Above all, the state of his body was a particular cause for comment, since he was a strong, well-built man, aged 43, and his body showed no obvious signs of illness or of murder. In fact, his corpse appeared so unaffected by his death that many people wished to see it, thinking that his end was in some way miraculous. On the other hand, Marlowe shows the final moments before his death, emphasizing his weakness caused by his imprisonment:

> *Edward*: I am too weak and feeble to resist.
> Assist me, sweet God, and receive my soul.[2]

Murimuth, whose contemporary chronicle was used as a source by many later writers, suggests that Edward was murdered by a 'trick' *(per cautelam)*. Perhaps Murimuth's phrase *per cautelam* became corrupted into *per cauterium* (a branding-iron), which gave rise to references to 'hot pokers' being used to kill him. Higden, writing not long after the actual events, gives much more detail and describes his dreadful death in which a hot cooking spit was inserted into his body 'through the secrete place posterialle'. Another writer referred to his abominable murder, 'being pierced with a heated iron spit in the hidden parts of his body'. Because his body appeared to be unmarked by signs of injury or illness, further rumours spread about his hideous murder. People said that, on the orders of Gurney and Maltravers, he was killed in a way that would leave no evidence, being pinned down by a heavy door, while his torturers pushed a cow's horn into his anus. They inserted a hot iron through the opening so that it went right inside him, but left no trace of burning on his skin.[3] Holinshed drew on these earlier chronicles and embroidered them with further details, dwelling on the horrors of the King's dungeon and its 'abominable stench'. He offered alternative opinions about the King's death and described the murderers entering the King's room while he was asleep and holding him down, either with a feather-bed or table, and then inserting a horn through which they passed a hot spit. In a second version, Holinshed suggested the use of a trumpet through which they passed a plumber's soldering-iron, 'rolled to and fro'. The resultant screams woke many in the town and castle of Berkeley.[4] These vivid, probably imaginary, descriptions of his murder also engage with the King's homosexuality and it seems that, in popular opinion, such a horrible death was regarded as somehow appropriate for him. The manner of his death mirrored his life.

As soon as the news of the King's death reached Parliament at Lincoln, royal ministers took charge and special arrangements were made for the care of the body. The corpse remained at Berkeley for a further month in the care of Thomas Berkeley and Maltravers, who continued to receive £5 a day, 'for the custody of the body'. Berkeley was paid by the Exchequer for the expenses of moving the body, for the cost of dyeing black the canvas that covered the hearse and for the expenses of members of his household who went with it to St Peter's Abbey, Gloucester. He was also recompensed for a silver vase to hold the King's heart and for masses sung in the castle chapel for the dead King. After the body was taken to Gloucester, the funeral was delayed for another two months and Edward was finally buried on December 20th 1327. The hearse was decorated with paintings of great gold lions, there was a massive use of gold leaf and there was a carved image of the former King, with a crown of gilded bronze on his head. The knights in attendance received new robes at the expense of Edward III.[5]

While Hidgen gave the dramatic details of his death, others presented a more conventional view:

> The deposed King died, either by a natural death or by the violence of another, and was buried at Gloucester and not in London among the other Kings, because he was deposed from reigning'.[6]

The version given in the *Anonimalle Chronicle* was even briefer, stating simply that Edward had become ill at Berkeley, died there and was buried at Gloucester.[7] The mysterious and unexpected manner of his death caused many people to look upon the King as a martyr, and they claimed that miracles occurred at his tomb, as happened at the tomb of the murdered Thomas of Lancaster. Because of the crush of people around his body, wanting to see it at Gloucester before it was buried, large oak timbers had to be used to form a barrier around it.[8] Ironically, the records of St. Peter's Abbey describe happier times in the past when Edward stayed there and was entertained by the Abbot. While the King sat at the Abbot's table, he noticed figures around the walls depicting his royal ancestors and enquired whether he was among them or not. The Abbot then replied that he hoped the King would reside in a more honourable place than at Gloucester. The chronicle of St Peter's claimed that other neighbouring religious houses in Bristol and Malmesbury refused to accept the body out of fear of Mortimer and Isabella. However, John Thoky, Abbot of St. Peter's, allowed the body to be taken in procession through the city and it was buried near the high altar. The place of burial was marked by a magnificent canopied tomb and, for many years after the funeral, a deep devotion to the King still remained. So many people began coming to Gloucester with offerings that the monks had enough money to complete a new aisle within six years. The new King also gave money, gold and jewels to the monks in honour of his father and, because of the great expenses incurred by his father's funeral, he granted St Peter's many privileges, principally reducing the amount of money payable by the monks to the Exchequer.[9]

Edward II was not forgotten and services were held throughout the country on the anniversary of his death. Fifty years later, Edward III gave express permission to the Abbot of Evesham to be absent from Parliament, except in an extreme emergency, on the grounds that he should be present every year with his monks, 'in solemn apparel at the anniversary of the late King, at Gloucester, where his body rests'. During 1385, Edward's great-grandson, Richard II, who was himself deposed and murdered 15 years later, wrote to the Pope requesting the canonization of Edward II, on the grounds that so many miracles had occurred at his tomb. His request was not granted but he visited Gloucester in 1390, where he met the Archbishop of Canterbury and other leading churchmen with the intention of making an investigation about the truth of the miracles and then putting in a further plea for canonization.[10] The canonization, however, never took place. But Richard II was aware of the uncomfortable precedent set by the deposition of Edward and his desire for his canonization may have been an attempt to raise his own status by association with a royal saint. The chronicle of Meaux Abbey also mentioned the desire of many people to regard Edward as a saint and martyr, following the precedent of Thomas of Lancaster. But the writer went on to declare that the great number of visitors to Edward's tomb or hundreds of miracles, even if they were authenticated, could never make him a saint, because of the wickedness of his life.[11] In spite of the elaborate public funeral and lavish gifts to St Peter's Abbey, there were rumours that Edward had escaped and was living abroad. There are suggestions that he managed to reach Ireland, then France, and ended his life as a hermit in Germany. Another version of events described how he escaped from Berkeley wearing the clothes of a servant, while the body of a porter was substituted for his and buried at Gloucester. Edward then supposedly remained in secret at Corfe Castle until he was able to travel to France and he ended his life as a recluse in a hermitage in Italy.[12]

Berkeley was acquitted of involvement in the King's death, but Gurney and Maltravers and their servants fled when charges of murder were made. The new King sent his officals to arrest them. They caught William of Kingsclere at Rochester, in Kent, and took him to the Tower; they arrested Richard Welle near Northampton and put him in Nottingham Castle, and delivered John le Spicer to the sheriff of London. The chief offenders escaped abroad but they were not safe from arrest. As the royal officials followed their trail, they caught John Tilly, a companion of Gurney, in Spain, and transferred him to the Castle of Malons in Gascony. They followed Gurney first to Spain and then to Italy, where he was finally caught. He was taken from Naples to Bologna by ship, but fell ill on the journey. His guards bought clothes and medicines for him but, in spite of their efforts, he died in France, at Bayonne. His captors brought his body back to England and eventually took it to Edward III at Berwick.[13] Maltravers was outlawed by Edward III and went to Germany, but he was later pardoned and his estates were restored to him.

Edward III had been crowned at Westminster by the Archbishop of Canterbury in February 1327 and a council of regency was set up, headed by Henry of Lancaster. Mortimer did not serve on the council but left others to present his views. The Queen regained the property that she had lost and acquired many of the jewels and plate and estates that had once belonged to the younger Despenser. Mortimer, too, received large grants of property, much of it in the form of lordships previously held by the Despensers and their associates. In addition, he took the office of Justice of Wales, which gave him extensive powers throughout the Principality and the Welsh Marches and, finally, he became Earl of March. He lived in great luxury and staged lavish tournaments to celebrate his high position. His greed was beginning to attract the kind of criticism that had formerly assailed the Despensers, 'exceeding Gavaston in foppery, and the Despensers in pride and cruelty'.[14] Mortimer's actions drove Lancaster and others to complain openly that the council of regency was ineffective against Mortimer and Isabella. Civil war threatened once more as Lancaster gathered a force of soldiers at Winchester. Mortimer, in retaliation, marched into the Earl's lands in Leicestershire and took possession of the city of Leicester. Edward III now faced a difficult situation. He owed his throne to his mother and Mortimer but, following the accession, Mortimer enjoyed virtually royal power. He had already conspired with Isabella to remove the Earl of Kent, the King's uncle, on the grounds that he might be a threat to their position. They had persuaded the Earl that Edward II was still alive but was being held prisoner at Corfe Castle. The Earl believed them and became involved in a plot to rescue him. As a result, he was arrested and executed for treason. Lancaster saw that a similar fate would be in store for him unless he persuaded the King to act against Mortimer. With the aid of two members of the Household, Richard Bury and William Montague, a plot was laid, with the connivance of the King. While the council was meeting at Nottingham in October 1327, Isabella and Mortimer were staying in the castle. They had taken the precaution of lodging in the strongest part of the castle and mounting a guard, while the Queen supposedly kept the keys of the castle under her pillow. But, with the help of the constable of the castle, Montague was shown a secret entrance through which he led a group of supporters, who were then joined by the King. They found Mortimer in his apartments; they killed his guards but held him and took him to the Tower, in spite of the pleas of Isabella to treat him with mercy. Parliament condemned him to death as a traitor and he was hanged at Tyburn, being the first nobleman to be hanged at a place of common execution.[15]

There were no charges against Isabella who was considered an innocent tool of the evil Mortimer. After the death of her husband she had taken over large amounts of his property, including his favourite house at Langley. She also acquired the castle at Guildford and the royal apartments nearby, Hadleigh Castle in Essex, Leeds Castle in Kent, from which she had once been excluded by Badlesmere, Odiham Castle, which Damory had formerly held, and the stronghold of Portchester Castle on the south coast. However, she was forced to hand over her property, receiving an annual allowance instead, and she took up residence at Castle Rising, Norfolk, with a considerable retinue of servants. The castle was her own property. The great square keep was surrounded by a deep ditch and high rampart, on which was built a strong wall with three towers. It is still a formidable fortress. Isabella was 36 years of age at the time and, from then on, she generally stayed out of politics and concentrated on more personal matters; she kept her status as Queen Mother and her son visited her from time to time. After two years, he restored to her the revenues of Ponthieu and Montreuil, which had been once granted to her by her husband. The

King paid her bills for food and wine, which included payments for turbot, lampreys and swans, 'for the former Queen'; she particularly enjoyed sturgeon and she received gifts of barrels of such luxury food from the people of King's Lynn. She rarely visited London, but was able to go on pilgrimages to the shrine of Our Lady at Walsingham, which was not far from Castle Rising. She also kept up her interests in hawking and in music. Her second son, John of Eltham, died in 1336, at the age of 20. Her elder daughter, Eleanor of Woodstock, married the Count of Gelderland, while her younger daughter, Joan of the Tower, married David Bruce, the heir to the throne of Scotland. When Isabella died, an inventory of her possessions recorded a chess-board made of crystal and jasper and books of historical romances, which included the story of the deeds of King Arthur, as well as a Bible and psalter. Her chapel at Castle Rising was magnificently decorated and, in her later years, Isabella joined a religious order.[16] She died in August 1358, at the age of 63, and was buried in London at the church of Greyfriars within Newgate, where Mortimer had been buried almost 30 years previously. She had contributed money to the building of the church and a fine alabaster tomb was built for her there. At her own request, she was buried in her wedding dress, with the silver casket containing her husband's heart at her side. She had outlived her husband by more than 30 years.[17]

XXIX EPILOGUE

A chronicler summed up the unhappy reign of Edward II soon after his death as a period of destruction rather than governance, resulting from the King's failure to obey the commands of his father. The writer blamed his careless attitude and disregard, which brought discord with his nobles and defeat by the Scots. He was criticized for relying on bad advice which led to the death of Thomas of Lancaster and of many others and finally to his own disgraceful deposition and murder. 'All this befell him because he scorned the words of his father and underrated the effects of his everlasting curse upon Gavaston'.[1]

His father had presented a powerful image. He had been a man of strong character who had commanded respect in both war and politics. After a reign lasting almost 35 years, he had come to embody a tradition of kingship, which people assumed his son would follow. But unlike his father, Edward II was bored by the traditional duties of a King and unable to fulfil his destiny. He sowed the seeds of his own destruction by treating great men with contempt, preferring the company of workmen. To have a ruler who lacked dignity became an unacceptable contradiction to those who tried to govern.

In the eyes of his contemporaries, the evils of his reign stemmed from his obsessive attachment to Gavaston, which clouded his judgement. However, the overriding cause was the King's own unstable personality. He usually followed the easiest path and agreed with the last person who spoke to him, with the result that his opinions fluctuated from hour to hour. People distrusted his decisions and, in the words of a present-day historian, Edward II was as troublesome to his friends as to his enemies.[2] He followed his own inclinations to a degree that puzzled those who encountered him. For example, he might conduct business while out hunting and he was happy to hold a party on a working-barge on the Thames, while buying cabbages from the gardeners on the banks to make his soup. He took pleasure in light-hearted pastimes and would throw coins to play Heads or Tails or pay his painter to dance on the table for the general amusement. He was interested in country pursuits and architecture, he loved music and enjoyed gambling.[3] He made occasional attempts to conform to the accepted pattern of behaviour for a King which irritated his nobles to an even greater degree, as he showed them that he could rule effectively, but chose not to. He also chose to flaunt his homosexuality at a time when society was becoming increasingly homophobic. An assessment of his personality suggests that he was an implusive and unpredictable man who was easily bored, a trait that allowed his friends to gain influence by manipulating his boredom to their advantage. Edward's disdain for government allowed, or forced, others to assume power. Some were individuals, such as his wife, his friends, or his relations; others formed groups, such as leading churchmen, nobles and justices. Among these changing alliances, rival parties competed for land, wealth and high office.

On the other hand, Edward's loyalty and generosity to those who pleased or amused him was boundless and, when he was stirred to action by the threat of war or when his friends were in danger, he reacted energetically and forcefully. All this suggests a reactive personality. He responded to boredom by looking for entertainment and needed threats of danger to spur him on to fight. Without such motivation, he seemed generally incapable of making plans or showing foresight. Even when he was in a powerful position after destroying his enemies at Boroughbridge, he could not take advantage of his victory:

> He had not learned to make or manage his friends; he could not govern and they misgoverned. To a great extent the fall of Edward II was due to his incapacity for government.[4]

His problems were increased by a wife who eventually despaired of his instability and was forced to assert her own will. She was a beautiful and intelligent woman of strong character, who accompanied him on his travels and took an active part in politics. For a while, she seemed able to fill the vacuum left by the death of Gavaston, but soon became a victim of the Despensers' ambitions. She accepted the King's homosexual preferences, but humiliation at the hands of the Despensers proved to be the last straw. She finally refused to accept a compliant role and found many to support her courageous acts of desertion, then invasion.

The combination of the King's inability, or unwillingness, to govern and a series of natural disasters and economic problems brought inevitable failure. His reign was dogged with seemingly everlasting warfare, but he lacked the money and resources to achieve a lasting victory. The Exchequer was forced to impose severe taxation but, because of the problems of collection, very little revenue reached its destination. It was an intolerable situation, made worse by famine and disease. Contemporaries saw his reign as a time when corn was dear, fields were empty and hunger was all around. The whole country was full of strife.[5]

Events in London were probably more extreme than in other places, but they serve to illustrate the instability of the time, as citizens experienced sudden changes from favour to persecution, depending on the King's state of mind. When he was in a good mood, he made grants and concessions to the Londoners, which were soon threatened when he needed money. On a larger scale, the overall political and financial difficulties caused widespread unrest and lawlessness.[6]

Because of his sudden and mysterious death, he was regarded as a martyr and people flocked to pay their respects at his tomb. A chronicler who gave a brief account of his reign emphasized this aspect:

> 1307: On the 30th day of January at Westminster was crowned Edward of Caernarvon, he was murdered in Berkeley Castle and he was buried at Gloucester, where many miracles occur every year.[7]

In spite of attempts to canonize Edward, his reputation as a monarch has been universally condemned, perhaps rivalled only by King John. Whereas John has been criticized for being 'no Christian', Edward, described as 'a passionate and difficult man', has incurred what may be considered the ultimate insult for a King, of failing to be a 'gentleman'.[8]

NOTES

Introduction
1. Denholm-Young, *Life of Edward*, p. 40.
2. Hutchison, 'Edward II and his Minions', pp. 542-9.
3. Babington, *Polychronicon*, 8, p. 298.
4. Taylor, *The Universal Chronicle*, pp. 1-2.
5. Holinshed, *Chronicles of England*, 2, pp. 546-7. *Blanketing*-tossing a person in a blanket as a playful form of punishment.
6. Forker, *Edward the Second*.
7. Tout, *The Place of Edward II*, pp. 9-11.
8. Prestwich, *The Three Edwards*, p. 79.
9. Chaplais, *Piers Gaveston*, p. 3.
10. Rutherford, *Sarum*, p. 743.
11. Druon, *The Iron King*, p. 24.
12. Tout, *The Place of Edward II*, pp. 9-11.
13. *Ibid.*, *The English Civil Service*.
14. Gransden, 'The Chronicles of Medieval England and Scotland', 16, pp. 135-7.

Chapter I
1. Murray Smith, *The Roll-Call*, p. 222.
2. Luard, *Flores Historiarum*, 3, p. 59.
3. Colvin, *History of the King's Works*, 1, pp. 369-95.
4. Johnstone, *Edward of Caernarvon*, p. 7.
5. Stubbs, *Chronicles*, 1, p. 92.
6. BL. Cott., Nero, C, VIII, f. 85. Johnstone, *Edward of Caernarvon*, p. 9.
7. BL. Cott., Nero, C, VIII, f. 141. *Cal. Close Rolls 1307-13*, p. 581. *Cal. Pat. Rolls 1307-13*, pp. 341; 510. *Cal. Pat. Rolls 1317-21*, p. 251.
8. Byerly, *Records of Wardrobe and Household*.
9. *Cal. Docs. Scot.*, 2, p. 109.
10. Green, *Lives of the Princesses*, 2, pp. 409-23. *Cal. Pat. Rolls 1307-13*, p. 510. Johnstone, *Edward of Caernarvon*, pp.24-5.
11. Cal. Close Rolls 1288-96, p. 502. Johnstone, *Edward of Caernarvon*, pp. 15-17.
12. Byerly, *Records of Wardrobe and Household*.

13. Colvin, *History of the King's Works*, 2, p. 1007.
14. PRO. E101 368/8 f. 5; SC11 279. Colvin, *History of the King's Works*, 2, pp. 970-7. Johnstone, *Edward of Caernarvon* p. 29. RCHME, *Hertfordshire*, p. 135. Page, *VCH.*, *Hertfordshire*, 2, p. 135.
15. Luard, *Ann. Monast.*, 3, pp. 392-3.
16. Riley, *Rishanger*, p. 397.
17. *Cal. Pat. Rolls 1301-7*, p. 31.
18. Luard, *Ann. Monast.*, 3. pp. 362-3.
19. Colvin, *History of the King's Works*, 1, pp. 479-86. Parsons, *Eleanor of Castile*.
20. Johnstone, *Edward of Caernarvon*, pp. 23-4.

Chapter II
1. *Cal. Pat. Rolls 1281-92*, p. 327.
2. Stones, *Anglo-Scottish Relations*, p. xxiv.
3. *Cal. Docs. Scot.*, 2, pp. 144-5.
4. *Ibid.*, pp. 106-8.
5. *Cal. Pat. Rolls 1281-92*, pp. 327; 386. Hardy, *Rymer*, 1, p. 110.
6. Stones, *Anglo-Scottish Relations*, p. xxiv.
7. Hardy, *Rymer*, 1, p. 128.

Chapter III
1. Graham, *Register of Robert Winchelsey*, 1, pp. 201-7.
2. Levison, 'St Edmundsbury Chronicle', p. 75.
3. Wright, *Chronicle of Langtoft*, 2, p. 324.
4. Topham, *Liber Quot.*, p. 169.
5. Wright, *Roll of Caerlaverock*.
6. Riley, *Rishanger*, p. 440. Topham, *Liber Quot.*, p. 70.
7. Bradbury, *Medieval Seige*, p. 143. Topham, *Liber Quot.*, p. 65.
8. Topham, *Liber Quot.*, pp. 166-7.
9. PRO. E101 360/10.

Chapter IV
1. *Cal. Charter Rolls 1300-26*, p. 6. *Cal. Pat. Rolls 1292-1301*, p. 576.
2. BL. Add. MSS. 7966A f. 155.
3. Johnstone, *Edward of Caernarvon*, p. 61.
4. *Ibid.*, p. 62.
5. Luard, *Flores Historiarum*, 3, p. 304.
6. Johnstone, *Letters of Edward*, p. 11.
7. Dimok, *Opera Giraldi Cambrensis*, 6, pp. 186-7.
8. BL. Add. MSS. 22923 f. 5. Johnstone, *Letters of Edward*, p. 114.
9. Tout, *Chapters*, 2, p. 173.

10. *Cal. Close Rolls 1307-13*, p. 180.
11. Johnstone, *Edward of Caernarvon*, p. 69. *Cal. Close Rolls 1302-7*, p. 64.
12. Hardy, *Rymer*, 1, p. 131.
13. Johnstone, *Edward of Caernarvon*, p. 73.
14. BL. Add. MSS. 7966A ff. 100-2.
15. PRO. E101 9/23. *Cal. Pat. Rolls 1292-1301*, pp. 593-6. Tout, *Chapters*, 2, p. 133.
16. Luard, *Flores Historiarum*, 3, p. 109.
17. Johnstone, *Edward of Caernarvon*, p. 80. *Cal. Docs. Scot.*, 2, p. 321.
18. Maxwell, *Chronicle of Lanercost*, p. 200. *Cal. Docs. Scot.*, 2, p. 319.
19. *Cal. Docs. Scot.*, 2, pp. 312-3.
20. Johnstone, *Edward of Caernarvon*, p. 81. *Cal. Docs. Scot.*, 2, p. 323.
21. Luard, *Flores Historiarum*, 3, p. 111.
22. PRO. E101 363/18. Johnstone, *Edward of Caernarvon*, p. 85.
23. BL. Add. MSS. 8835 f. 7. PRO. E101 363/18.
24. *Cal. Docs. Scot.*, 2, pp. 366-70.
25. Luard, *Flores Historiarum*, 3, p. 313.
26. Lumby, *Knighton*, p. 383.
27. Luard, *Flores Historiarum*, 3, p. 119.
28. Bradbury, *Medieval Seige*, p. 144.
29. Johnstone, *Letters of Edward*.
30. *Cal. Pat. Rolls 1301-7*, p. 428.
31. *Cal. Close Rolls 1302-7*, p. 434.
32. Luard, *Flores Historiarum*, 3, pp. 131-2.
33. Wright, *Langtoft*, 2, p. 369.
34. BL. Add. MSS. 22923. *Cal. Close Rolls 1302-7*, pp. 386; 400; 408. Johnstone, *Edward of Caernarvon*, p. 115. Maxwell, *Chronicle of Lanercost*, pp. 204-5. Chaplais, *Piers Gaveston*, pp. 26-7. Rothwell, *Chronicle of Walter of Guisborough*, p. 380.
35. Forker, *Edward the Second*, p. 141.
36. Chaplais, *Piers Gaveston*, pp. 30-4. Page, *VCH.*, Cornwall, 1, pp. 522-62.
37. Rothwell, *Chronicle of Walter of Guisborough*, p. 383.
38. Forker, *Edward the Second*, p. 151.

Chapter V
1. Babington, *Polychronicon*, 8, p. 299. Holinshed, *Chronicles*, 2, p. 547.
2. Forker, *Edward the Second*, p. 144.
3. Chaplais, *Piers Gaveston*, pp. 5-45. Hamilton, *Piers Gaveston*, p. 30. Topham, *Liber Quot.*, p. 179.

4. BL. Cott., Cleopatra, D, IX, ff. 83-5. Johnstone, *Edward of Caernarvon*, pp. 42-3.
5. Stubbs, *Chronicles*, 1, p. 138.
6. Colvin, *History of the King's Works*, 2, p. 206.
7. *Cal. Close Rolls 1302-7*, p. 342. Johnstone, *Letters of Edward*, pp. xlii-l.
8. Johnstone, *Letters of Edward*, p. 70.
9. Blaauw, 'Letters of Edward', pp. 80-98. Johnstone, *Edward of Caernarvon*, pp. 96-101.
10. *Cal. Close Rolls 1302-7*, pp. 526-7. Hardy, *Rymer*, 1, p. 143.
11. Johnstone, *Edward of Caernarvon*, p. 123.
12. Rothwell, *Chronicle of Walter of Guisborough*, p. 382.
13. BL. Add. MSS. 22923 ff. 6-15.
14. Johnstone, *Edward of Caernarvon*, p. 124.
15. Luard, *Flores Historiarum*, 3. p. 229.
16. Bond, *Chronicle of Melsa*, 2, p. 355. Boswell, *Christianity*, pp. 298-301.
17. Chaplais, *Piers Gaveston*, p. 7.
18. Boswell, *Christianity*, pp. 284-5. Brundage, *Law, Sex and Christian Society*, pp. 472-4. Frolich, *St Anselm*, 1, p. 249.
19. Stubbs, *Chronicles*, 1, p. 190.
20. Chaplais, *Piers Gaveston*, pp. 10; 21.
21. BL. Stowe MS. 553 f. 27. Blackley, 'Adam, Bastard Son', pp. 76-7.

Chapter VI
1. Denholm-Young, *Life of Edward*, p. 40.
2. BL. Add. MSS. 35093 f. 41.
3. *Cal. Close Rolls 1307-13*, p. 53.
4. Denholm-Young, *Life of Edward*, p. 1.
5. BL. Add. MSS. 35093.
6. Denholm-Young, *Life of Edward*, p. 2.
7. Colvin, *History of the King's Works*, 2, pp. 179-80.
8. Beardwood, *Trial of Walter Langeton*, pp. 1-3.
9. Stubbs, *Chronicles*, 1, p. 258.
10. Phillips, *Aymer de Valence*, p. 25.
11. *Cal. Close Rolls 1307-13*, p. 18.
12. Macaulay, *Chronicles of Froissart*, p. 3.
13. Stubbs, *Chronicles*, 1, p. 258.
14. Chaplais, *Piers Gaveston*, pp. 41-2.
15. Denholm-Young, *Life of Edward*, p. 3.
16. Stubbs, *Chronicles*, 1, pp. 258-9.
17. Forker, *Edward the Second*, p. 173.
18. Luard, *Flores Historiarum*, pp. 139; 229.
19. Phillips, *Aymer de Valence*, pp. 25-8.

Chapter VII

1. *Cal. Close Rolls 1307-13*, p. 52.
2. Colvin, *History of the King's Works*, 1, pp. 505-7. Devon, *Issues of the Exchequer*, pp. 120-2. Hardy, *Rymer*, 1, p. 146. Strickland, *Queens of England*, 1, p. 473.
3. Stubbs, *Chronicles*, 1, p. 260.
4. Hardy, *Rymer*, 1, p. 150.
5. *Cal. Close Rolls 1307-13*, p. 53.
6. Hardy, *Rymer*, 1, p. 150.
7. Stubbs, *Chronicles*, 1, p. 262.
8. Luard, *Flores Historiarum*, 3, p. 331.
9. Stubbs, *Chronicles*, 1, pp. 261-2.
10. Luard, *Flores Historiarum*, 3, p. 331.
11. *Ibid.*, p. 229.
12. Chaplais, *Piers Gaveston*, p. 44. Tuck, *Crown and Nobility*, p. 54.

Chapter VIII

1. Riley, *Chronicle of Thomas Walsingham*, 1, p. 115.
2. Stubbs, *Chronicles*, 2, p.33.
3. Denholm-Young, *Life of Edward*, p. 4. Stubbs, *Chronicles*, 1, p. 263.
4. Strickland, *Lives of Queens of England*, 1, p. 480.
5. Tuck, *Crown and Nobility*, pp. 55-6.
6. Hingeston-Randolph, *Register of Walter de Stapledon*, pp. 11-12.
7. Stubbs, *Chronicles*, 1, pp. 154-5.
8. *Cal. Charter Rolls 1300-26*, pp. 110-11. *Cal. Pat. Rolls 1307-13*, p. 78. Hardy, *Rymer*, 1, p. 152.
9. Chaplais, *Piers Gaveston*, p. 51.
10. Stubbs, *Chronicles*, 1, p. 263.
11. Denholm-Young, *Life of Edward*, p. 4.
12. Hamilton, *Piers Gaveston*, pp. 58-60.
13. Hardy, *Rymer*, 1, p. 151.
14. *Cal. Pat. Rolls 1307-13*, p. 74.
15. Hardy, *Rymer*, 1, p. 151. *Cal. Gascon Rolls 1307-13*, pp. 56; 113.
16. Tout, *The Place of Edward II*, pp. 36-7.
17. Hamilton, *Piers Gaveston*, pp. 58-9.
18. Denholm-Young, *Life of Edward*, pp. 6-7. Tuck, *Crown and Nobility*, p. 57.
19. Denholm-Young, *Life of Edward*, p. 8.
20. *Cal. Docs, Scot.*, 3, p. 20.
21. Denholm-Young, *Life of Edward*, pp. 8-9.
22. *Ibid.*, p. 9.
23. McKisack, *The Fourteenth Century*, p. 10.

24. Tout, *Place of Edward II*, pp. 85-7. *Rot. Parl.*, 1, pp. 381-6.
25. Graham, *Register of Robert Winchelsey*, 2, p. 1043.

Chapter IX

1. Tuck, *Crown and Nobility*, p. 52.
2. Denholm-Young, *Life of Edward*, p. 11.
3. BL. Cott., Nero, C, VIII, ff. 8; 13; 42.
4. Denholm-Young, *Life of Edward*, p. 11.
5. BL. Cott., Nero, C, VIII, f. 65.
6. *Ibid.*, ff. 2-58.
7. *Cal. Chancery Warrants*, 1, p. 369.

Chapter X

1. *Stat. Realm*, 1, pp. 157-67. McKisack, *The Fourteenth Century*, pp. 9-13.
2. Stubbs, *Chronicles*, 1, p. 202. Mc Kisack, *The Fourteenth Century*. pp. 14-17.
3. Childs and Taylor, *Anon. Chron.*, p. 85. Maddicott, *Thomas of Lancaster*, p. 117. Stubbs, *Chronicles*, 1, p. 270.
4. Denholm-Young, *Life of Edward*, p. 21.
5. Tout, *Place of Edward II*, p. 28.

Chapter XI

1. Tuck, *Crown and Nobility*, pp. 55-6.
2. McKisack, *The Fourteenth Century*, pp. 291-2. Upton-Ward, *The Rule of the Templars*, pp. 1-9.
3. Maxwell, The *Chronicle of Lanercost*, p. 107.
4. Rothwell, The *Chronicle of Walter of Guisborough*, pp. 387-95.
5. Prestwich, *Edward I*, p. 481. *Cal. Close Rolls 1302-7*, p. 67.
6. *Cal. Close Rolls 1302-7*, pp. 14; 48.
7. *Ibid.*, pp. 189; 285; 365. Graham, *Register of Robert Winchelsey*, 2, p. 1004.
8. Stubbs, *Chronicles*, 1, pp. 179-98.
9. BL. Cott., Nero, C, VIII, f. 50.

Chapter XII

1. Denholm-Young, *Life of Edward*, p. 21.
2. *Cal. Close Rolls 1307-13*, pp. 448-9.
3. Hardy, *Rymer*, 1, p. 154. Tout, *Place of Edward II*, pp. 96-7.
4. BL. Cott., Nero, C, VIII, ff. 136-41. Blackley and Hermansen, *Household Book of Isabella*.
5. BL. Cott., Nero, C, VIII, f. 84.

6. *Ibid.*, Chaplais, *Piers Gaveston*, p. 78. Green, *Lives of the Princesses*, 2, p. 433.
7. *Cal. Pat. Rolls 1307-13*, p. 413.
8. Tout, *The Place of Edward II*, pp. 97-8.
9. McKisack, *The Fourteenth Century*, pp. 23-4.
10. Denholm-Young, *The Life of Edward*, p. 22.
11. Stubbs, *Chronicles*, 1, p. 204.
12. McKisack, *The Fourteenth Century*, p. 25.
13. BL. Cott., Nero, C, VIII, f. 86.
14. Riley, *Chronicle of Thomas Walsingham*, 1, p. 131.
15. BL. Cott., Nero, C, VIII, f. 58. *Cal. Close Rolls 1307-13*, p. 416. *Cal. Fine Rolls 1307-19*, p. 129.
16. Denholm-Young, *Life of Edward*, p. 24. Luard, *Flores Historiarum*, 3, pp. 150-1. Phillips, *Aymer de Valence*, p. 33.
17. Luard, *Flores Historiarum*, 3, pp. 152-3. McKisack, *The Fourteenth Century*, p. 26. Stubbs, *Chronicles*, 1, pp. 206-7.
18. Stubbs, *Chronicles*, 2, pp. 39; 43-4. Davies, *Baronial Opposition*, App. no. 138.
19. Denholm-Young, *Life of Edward*, p. 28.
20. *Ibid.*, pp. 28-9. Stubbs, *Chronicles*, 1, p. 207.
21. Wright, *Political Songs*, pp. 258-61.
22. BL. Cott., Nero, C, VIII, f. 63. Denholm-Young, *Life of Edward*, p. 30.
23. PRO. E101 375/15-16. Stubbs, *Chronicles*, 1, p. 273.
24. BL. Cott., Nero, C, VIII, ff. 83-5.
25. Stubbs, *Chronicles*, 1, p. 208; 2, p. 44.
26. Hardy, *Rymer*, 1, p. 172. Stubbs, *Chronicles*, 1, p. 209.

Chapter XIII
1. Chaplais, *Piers Gaveston*, pp. 90-108.
2. Riley, *Chronicle of Thomas Walsingham*, 1, p. 134. Edwards, 'Bishops', p. 324.
3. Stubbs, *Chronicles*, 1, pp. 210-11.
4. Hamilton, *Piers Gaveston*, p. 105-6.
5. Stubbs, *Chronicles*, 1, pp. 211-12.
6. *Ibid.*, pp. 215-7.
7. *Ibid.*, pp. 272-3.

Chapter XIV
1. *Cal. Charter Rolls 1300-26*, pp. 202-3.
2. *Cal. Pat. Rolls 1307-13*, p. 519.
3. Colvin, *History of the King's Works*, 1, p. 244. Stubbs, *Chronicles*, 1, p. 221.

4. Strickland, *Queens of England*, 1, pp. 482-4.
5. Hardy, *Rymer*, 1, p. 180.
6. Tout, *The Place of Edward II*, pp. 214-9.
7. Denholm-Young, The *Life of Edward*, p. 39.
8. Hardy, *Rymer*, 1, p. 180. Riley, *Chronicle of Thomas Walsingham*, 1, p. 136. Strickland, *Queens of England*, 1, p. 484.
9. Tout, *The Place of Edward II*, pp. 320-1.
10. Hardy, *Rymer*, 1, p. 155.
11. Denholm-Young, *Life of Edward*, p. 45.
12. *Ibid.*, pp. 39-40.
13. Riley, *Chronicle of Thomas Walsingham*, 1, pp. 138-9.
14. PRO. E101 375/9. *Cal. Pat. Rolls 1313-17*, p. 285. *Cal. Treaty Rolls*, p. 207.

Chapter XV
1. BL. Cott., Nero, C, VIII, f. 249.
2. *Cal. Docs. Scot.*, 3, pp. 65-6.
3. Dickinson and Duncan, *Scotland*, p. 165.
4. Denholm-Young, *Life of Edward*, pp. 50-1. Luard, *Flores Historiarum*, 3, p. 158.
5. *Cal. Close Rolls, 1313-17*, pp. 95; 103.
6. BL. Cott., Nero, C, VIII, ff. 209-12. Cooper, *History of Winchelsea*, pp. 62-3.
7. Wright, *Political Songs*, p. 263.
8. Maxwell, *Chronicle of Lanercost*, pp. 206-7.
9. Madox, *Exchequer*, 2, pp. 84-5. Johnstone, 'Eccentricities of Edward II', pp. 264-7.
10. Altschul, *A Baronial Family*, pp. 170-1. Waugh, *The Lordship*, p. 249.

Chapter XVI
1. *Cal. Pat. Rolls 1313-17*, p. 169. Hardy, *Rymer*, 1, p. 183. Hingeston-Randolph, *The Register of Walter de Stapledon*, p. xix.
2. Tout, *The Place of Edward II*, pp. 100-1.
3. Denholm-Young, *Life of Edward*, p. 59.
4. Stubbs, *Chronicles*, 1, p. 279.
5. Hardy, *Rymer*, 1, p. 185. Lucas, 'The Great European Famine', pp. 343-59. Stubbs, *Chronicles*, 1, p. 233.
6. PRO. E101 375/20.
7. Denholm-Young, *Life of Edward*, p. 60.
8. Maxwell, *Chronicle of Lanercost*, p. 230. Rothwell, *Chronicle of Walter of Guisborough*, p. 396.
9. Denholm-Young, *Life of Edward*, p. 61.

10. *Cal. Docs. Scot.*, 3, pp. 85-6. *Cal. Pat Rolls 1313-17*, p. 455. Rothwell, *Chronicle of Walter of Guisborough*, p. 397.
11. Denholm-Young, *Life of Edward*, p. 61.
12. BL. Nero, Cott., C, VIII, f. 269. Colvin, *History of the King's Works*, 2, pp. 918-19. Denholm-Young, *Life of Edward*, p. 62. Riley, *Chronicle of Thomas Walsingham*, 1, p. 173.
13. Hardy, *Rymer*, 1, p. 188.
14. Tout, *Place of Edward II*, pp. 104-5.
15. *Cal. Docs. Scot.*, 3, pp. 89-90.
16. *Ibid.*, p. 91.
17. *Ibid.*, p. 105.
18. Luard, *Flores Historiarum*, 3, p. 174. *Cal. Pat. Rolls 1313-17*, p. 455.
19. Stubbs, *Chronicles*, 1, p. 239.
20. Denholm-Young, *Life of Edward*, pp. 66-8. Hardy, *Rymer*, 1, pp. 187-8. *Stat. Realm*, 1, p. 162.
21. *Cal. Close Rolls 1313-18*, pp. 423-4. Denholm-Young, *Life of Edward*, pp. 70-5. Phillips, *Aymer de Valence*, pp. 102-3.
22. Denholm-Young, *Life of Edward*, pp. 74-5.
23. Hardy, *Rymer*, 1, p. 189.
24. Stubbs, *Chronicles*, 1, p. 237.
25. Luard, *Flores Historiarum*, 3, pp. 176-7.

Chapter XVII
1. Hardy, *Rymer*, 1, p. 189.
2. Strickland, *Queens of England*, 1, p. 458.
3. *Cal. Pat. Rolls 1317-21*, p. 331. Phillips, *Aymer de Valence*, pp. 107-11.
4. *Cal. Docs. Scot.*, 3, 101-2.
5. Luard, *Flores Historiarum*, 3, p. 178. Phillips, *Aymer de Valence*, p. 132.
6. *Cal. Pat. Rolls, 1313-17*, pp. 234; 237. Waugh, *The Lordship*, p. 249.
7. Altschul, *A Baronial Family*, pp. 170-1.
8. Stapleton, 'Summary of Wardrobe Accounts', pp. 337; 339.

Chapter XVIII
1. Luard, *Flores Historiarum*, 3. p. 179. Riley, *Chronicle of Thomas Walsingham*, 1, p. 148.
2. Stubbs, *Chronicles*, 2, pp. 50-2.
3. Denholm-Young, *Life of Edward*, p. 80.
4. *Cal. Papal Letters 1305-42*, pp. 438-9.
5. Riley, *Chronicle of Thomas of Walsingham*, 1, pp. 149-50.
6. Stubbs, *Chronicles*, 1, pp. 140-1.
7. Strickland, *Queens of England*, 1, p. 486.
8. Stapleton, 'Summary of Wardrobe Accounts', p. 344.

9.   Leader, *Cambridge*, pp. 78-80.
10. *Cal. Close Rolls 1313-18*, p. 477.
11. Hardy, *Rymer*, 1, p. 195.
12. Luard, *Flores Historiarum*, 3, pp. 181-2.
13. Stapleton, 'Summary of Wardrobe Accounts', p. 320.
14. Denholm-Young, *Life of Edward*, p. 81.
15. *Cal. Close Rolls 1313-18*, pp. 504-5. *Cal. Fine Rolls 1307-19*, p. 344. *Cal. Pat. Rolls 1317-21*, p. 46. Tout, *Place of Edward II*, pp. 108-9.

Chapter XIX
1.   Colvin, *History of the King's Works*, 2, p. 847. McKisack, *The Fourteenth Century*, p. 54. Phillips, *Aymer de Valence*, pp. 155-77.
2.   Tout, *Place of Edward II*, pp. 267-318.
3.   Strickland, *Queens of England*, 1, p. 485.
4.   Maddicott, *Thomas of Lancaster*, pp. 246-7.
5.   *Cal. Docs. Scot.*, 3, pp. 124-6.
6.   Skeat, *The Bruce*, 2, pp. 414-442.
7.   Riley, *Chronicle of Thomas Walsingham*, 1, pp. 155.
8.   Luard, *Flores Historiarum*, 3, p. 188.
9.   Denholm-Young, *Life of Edward*, pp. 95-6. Strickland, *Queens of England*, 1, p. 488.
10. Skeat, *The Bruce*, 2, pp. 131-8.
11. Maxwell, *Chronicle of Lanercost*, p. 239.
12. Denholm-Young, *Life of Edward*, p. 97.
13. Skeat, *The Bruce*, 2, pp. 320-21.
14. BL. Add. MSS. 17362.
15. Stubbs, *Chronicles*, 1, p. 286.
16. Luard, *Flores Historiarum*, 3, pp. 190-3.
17. BL. Add. MSS. 17362, f. 53. Denholm-Young, *Life of Edward*, pp. 103-4.
18. Colvin, *History of the King's Works*, 1, p. 508. Luard, *Flores Historiarum*, 3, p. 193.
19. *Ibid.*, p. 169.

Chapter XX
1.   Denholm-Young, *Life of Edward*, p. 104.
2.   Hingeston-Randolph, *Register of Walter de Stapledon*, p. xxiii. Luard, *Flores Historiarum*, 3, p. 191.
3.   *Cal. Pat. Rolls 1317-21*, pp. 425; 446-7; 452-3. Phillips, *Aymer de Valence*, p. 192.
4.   Stubbs, *Chronicles*, 1, p. 290.

5. Johnstone, 'Isabella', p. 213. Riley, *Chronicle of Thomas Walsingham*, 1, p. 158.
6. BL. Add. MSS., 17362 f. 11. BL. Cott., Nero, D, X, f. 110. Maddicott, *Thomas of Lancaster*, p. 255.
7. Luard, *Flores Historiarum*, 3, p. 191.
8. Davies, *Baronial Opposition*, pp. 470-2.
9. Pearce, *Register of Thomas de Cobham*, pp. 97-8.
10. BL. Cott., Nero, D, X, f. 110.
11. Phillips, *Aymer de Valence*, p. 198.

Chapter XXI
1. *Cal. Charter Rolls 1300-26*, pp. 398-9.
2. Knight, 'Newport Castle', p. 20.
3. *Cal. Pat. Rolls 1324-27*, p. 274. Tout, *Place of Edward II*, p. 211.
4. Phillips, *Aymer de Valence*, p. 220.
5. Davies, 'The Despenser War', p. 43.
6. Luard, *Flores Historiarum*, 3, pp. 194-6.
7. PRO. E101 15/2. *Cal. Close Rolls 1318-23*, pp. 292-3. *Cal. Pat. Rolls 1317-21*, p. 569.
8. Knight, 'Newport Castle', p. 20.
9. Davies, 'The Despenser War', pp. 43-4. Denholm-Young, *Life of Edward*, p. 111. Stubbs, *Chronicles*, 1, pp. 292-3. Tout, *Place of Edward II*, pp. 136-45.
10. *Cal. Close Rolls 1318-23*, pp. 541-6.
11. Denholm-Young, *Life of Edward*, p. 112.
12. *Cal. Pat. Rolls 1317-21*, p. 128.
13. Maddicott, *Thomas of Lancaster*, pp. 269-79.
14. *Cal. Close Rolls 1318-23*, pp. 492-5. *Stat. Realm*, 1, p. 181.
15. Denholm-Young, *Life of Edward*, pp. 115-6. Luard, *Flores Historiarum*, 3, p. 198. Stubbs, *Chronicles*, 1, p. 297.
16. Babington, *Polychronicon*, 8, p. 311.
17. Phillips, *Aymer de Valence*, p. 216. Riley, *Chronicle of Thomas Walsingham*, 1, pp. 161-2.
18. Bond, *Chronicle of Melsa*, 2, p. 339. Denholm-Young, *Life of Edward*, pp. 116-7.

Chapter XXII
1. *Cal. Close Rolls 1318-23*, pp. 410; 510-1. *Cal. Pat. Rolls 1321-24*, p. 37. Stubbs, *Chronicles*, 2, pp. 70-2.
2. Hardy, *Rymer*, 1, p. 213. Stubbs, *Chronicles*, 1, p. 304.
3. Buck, *Politics, Finance and the Church*, p. 137.
4. Luard, *Flores Historiarum*, 3, p. 345.

5. *Cal. Close Rolls 1318-23*, pp. 511-2.
6. Luard, *Flores Historiarum*, 3, p. 345.
7. Wright, *Political Songs*, pp. 268-9.
8. Childs and Taylor, *Anon. Chron.*, p. 109. McKisack, *The Fourteenth Century*, pp. 69-70.
9. BL. Cott., Cleopatra, D, IX, ff. 83-5. *Cal. Close Rolls 1318-23*, pp. 541-6; 557-8. Babington, *Polychronicon*, 8, p. 315. Haskins, 'A Chronicle', pp. 79-80.

Chapter XXIII
1. Riley, *Liber Cust.*, p. 409. Strickland, *Queens of England*, 1, p. 492.
2. Strickland, *Queens of England*, 1, p. 493.
3. *Cal. Close Rolls 1318-23*, p. 546. Tout, *Place of Edward II*, pp. 154-5.
4. Colvin, *History of the King's Works*, 2, pp. 667-9.
5. PRO. E101 15/2; 379/4. Fryde, 'The Deposits', pp. 347-8.
6. PRO. SC6 1145-8. Buck, 'The Reform of the Exchequer', pp. 241-60. Hall, *Red Book of the Exchequer*, 3, pp. 849-969. Heath, *Church and Realm*, pp. 98-9. Tout, *Chapters*, 2, pp. 337-345.
7. Hardy, *Rymer*, 1, p. 215.
8. Broome, 'Exchequer Migrations', pp. 294-300.
9. BL. Stowe MS. 553 ff. 119-124.
10. *Ibid.*, f. 45.
11. *Ibid.*, f. 27. Blackley, 'Adam, Bastard Son', pp. 76-7.
12. *Cal. Docs. Scot.*, 3, pp. 146-8.
13. Riley, *Chronicle of Thomas Walsingham*, 1, pp. 166-7.
14. BL. Stowe MS. 553 f. 125.
15. *Ibid.*, f. 34.
16. *Ibid.*, f. 147.
17. Luard, *Flores Historiarum*, 3, p. 209.
18. *Cal. Pat. Rolls 1321-24*, p. 269.
19. Riley, *Chronicle of Thomas Walsingham*, 1, p. 167.
20. Latham, *Memoranda Rolls 1326-7*, p. 151.
21. Hardy, *Rymer*, 1, p. 219.
22. Chaplais, *War of St Sardos*, pp. x-xxi.

Chapter XXIV
1. Childs and Taylor, *Anon. Chron.*, p. 117. Hardy, *Rymer*, 1, p. 190. Stones, 'Roger Mortimer's Escape', pp. 97-8.
2. PRO. E 101 492/21. *Cal. Close Rolls 1318-23*, pp. 656-7. *Cal. Pat Rolls 1321-4*, p. 234. Hardy, *Rymer*, 1, p. 220.
3. *Cal. Pat. Rolls 1321-24*, pp. 337-43. Tupling, *South Lancashire*, pp. lii-iii.

4. *Cal. Pat. Rolls 1321-24*, pp. 364-7. Riley, *Chronicle of Thomas Walsingham*, 1, pp. 170-1.
5. Macaulay, *Froissart*, p. 4.
6. Tout, *Place of Edward II*, p. 140.
7. Hardy, *Rymer*, 1, p. 226.
8. *Cal. Pat. Rolls 1321-24*, pp. 328; 398. Riley, *Chronicle of Thomas Walsingham*, 1, pp. 172-3.
9. *Cal. Close Rolls 1323-27*, p. 72. Sayles, 'Formal Judgement', p. 63.

Chapter XXV
1. Macaulay, *Froisssart*, pp. 4-5. Sheppard, *Canterbury Letters*, 1, pp. 169-71.
2. *Cal. Pat. Rolls 1324-27*, pp. 166-71.
3. BL. Add. MSS. 26891 ff. 31-2. Riley, *Chronicle of Thomas Walsingham*, 1, pp. 176-7.
4. *Cal. Close Rolls 1318-23*, pp. 11; 22.
5. PRO. SC6 1148/13.
6. *Cal. Pat. Rolls 1317-21*, pp. 115; 132.
7. Colvin, *History of the King's Works*, 2, pp. 994-5.
8. Buck, *Politics, Finance and the Church*, pp. 156-7. Colvin, *History of the King's Works*, 2, pp. 783-7. Riley, *Chronicle of Thomas Walsingham*, 1, p. 178.
9. *Cal. Close Rolls 1323-27*, pp. 576-82. Hardy, *Rymer*, 1, pp. 233-4.
10. *Cal. Close Rolls 1323-27*, p. 171.
11. PRO. E101 17/211-13.
12. PRO. E101 531/17. Colvin, *History of the King's Works*, 2, p. 724. Latham, *Memoranda Rolls 1326-27*, pp. 363; 368.
13. BL. Cott., Faustina, B, V, ff. 45-6. Buck, *Politics, Finance and the Church*, p. 158.
14. *Cal. Close Rolls 1323-27*, pp. 576-82. Hardy, *Rymer*, 1, p. 234.
15. Denholm-Young, *Life of Edward*, pp. 143-5.
16. Riley, *Chronicle of Thomas Walsingham*, 1, p. 178.
17. Macaulay, *Froissart*, p. 6.

Chapter XXVI
1. Devon, *Issues of the Exchequer*, p. 18. Raine, *Northern Registers*, p. 332.
2. *Cal. Close Rolls 1323-27*, pp. 640-4. *Cal. Pat. Rolls 1324-27*, pp. 308-10. Fryde, *Tyranny*, pp. 183-4.
3. Riley, *Chronicle of Thomas Walsingham*, 1, p. 179.
4. Aungier, *French Chronicle of London*, p. 51.
5. *Cal. Close Rolls 1323-27*, p. 655. Fryde, *Tyranny*, p. 185.

6. Riley, *Chronicle of Thomas Walsingham*, 1, p. 180. Stubbs, *Chronicles*, 1, p. 315.
7. Riley, *Chronicle of Thomas Walsingham*, 1, pp. 180-1.
8. Stubbs, *Chronicles*, 1, p. 315.
9. BL. Add. MSS. 26891. *Cal. Close Rolls 1323-27*, pp. 650-1. *Cal. Pat. Rolls 1324-27*, pp. 325-8.
10. Aungier, *French Chronicle of London*, pp. 51-5. Stubbs, *Chronicles*, 1, p. 316.
11. Du Boulay, *Lordship of Canterbury*, p. 115.
12. *Cal. Pat. Rolls 1324-27*, p. 337. Aungier, *French Chronicle of London*, p. 53. Riley, *Chronicle of Thomas Walsingham*, 1, pp. 181-2.
13. *Cal. Pat. Rolls 1324-27*, pp. 326-32. Luard, *Flores Historiarum*, 3, p. 233.
14. Stubbs, *Chronicles*, 1, pp. 314-8.
15. Forker, *Edward the Second*, p. 253.
16. *Cal. Fine Rolls 1319-27*, p. 422. *Cal. Pat. Rolls 1324-27*, pp. 333-7.
17. *Cal. Pat. Rolls 1324-27*, pp. 334-7. Hardy, *Rymer*, 1, p. 237. Ormrod, 'Edward II at Neath', pp. 107-12.
18. *Cal. Close Rolls 1323-27*, p. 655.
19. Luard, *Flores Historiarum*, 3, p. 234.
20. PRO. E142 56. Boswell, *Christianity*, p. 300. Macaulay, *Froissart*, p. 11. Riley, *Chronicle of Thomas Walsingham*, 1, pp. 183-5. Stubbs, *Chronicles*, 1, pp. 320-1.

Chapter XXVII
1. *Cal. Close Rolls 1323-27*, pp. 621-9; 677-9.
2. Maxwell, *Chronicle of Lanercost*, pp. 253-5.
3. *Cal. Close Rolls 1327-30*, p. 1. Hardy, *Rymer*, 1, p. 238.
4. Riley, *Chronicle of Thomas Walsingham*, 1, pp. 186-7. Stubbs, *Chronicles*, 1, p. 324.
5. *Cal. Pat. Rolls 1327-30*, pp. 27; 43-57.
6. BL. Harl., 46 A43. Hardy, *Rymer*, 1, pp. 241-2.
7. *Cal. Pat. Rolls 1327-30*, pp. 156-7. Forker, *Edward the Second*, p. 293. Hardy, *Rymer*, 1, p. 243. Stow, *Chronicles of England*, pp. 355-6. Tanquerey, 'The Conspiracy of Thomas Dunheved', pp. 119-124. Tout, *Collected Papers*, 3, pp. 145-90.

Chapter XXVIII
1. Strickland, *Queens of England*, 1, p. 524.
2. Forker, *Edward the Second*, p. 312.
3. BL. Cott., Faustina, B, VI, f. 81. BL. Cott., Nero, D, X, f. 114. Babington, *Polychronicon*, 8, p. 325. Riley, *Chronicle of Thomas of Walsingham*, 1, p. 189. Thompson, *Murimuth*, pp. 53-4.

4.   Holinshed, *Chronicles*, 2, p. 587.
5.   Hart, *History of St Peter's Abbey*, 1, pp. 44-5. Tout, *Collected Papers*, 3, pp. 169-70.
6.   Maxwell, *Chronicle of Lanercost.*
7.   Childs and Taylor, *Anon. Chron.* p. 135.
8.   BL. Add. MSS. 25459 ff. 173-9.
9.   Hart, *History of St Peter's Abbey*, 1, pp. 44-7.
10. *Cal. Close Rolls 1374-77*, p. 470. Hardy, *Rymer*, 1, p. 244. Hector and Harvey, *Westminster Chronicle*, pp. 159; 437-9.
11. Bond, *Chronicle of Melsa*, 2, p. 355.
12. Cuttino and Lyman, 'Where is Edward II?', pp. 522-39. Tout, *Collected Papers*, 3, pp. 145-190.
13. BL. Add. MSS. 25459 f. 164.
14. Strickland, *Queens of England*, 1, p. 530.
15. Childs and Taylor, *Anon. Chron.*, p. 145. Riley, *Chronicle of Thomas Walsingham*, 1, p. 193.
16. Hist. MSS. Comm., 11th Rep. App. pt. 3, pp. 214-8.
17. Fryde, *Tyranny*, p. 202. Johnstone, 'Isabella', pp. 208-18.

Chapter XXIX
1.   Riley, *Chronicle of Thomas Walsingham*, 1, pp. 114-16.
2.   Phillips, *Aymer de Valence*, p. 147.
3.   *Cal. Close Rolls 1313-18*, p. 406. Strickland, *Queens of England*, 1, p. 520.
4.   Stubbs, *Chronicles*, 1, p. cxiii.
5.   Eckhardt, *Castleford*, 2, p. 1065.
6.   Aungier, *French Chronicle of London.*
7.   BL. Cott., Tiberius, E, VIII.
8.   Fryde, *Tyranny*, p. 15. Johnstone, 'The Eccentricities of Edward II', pp. 264-7.

BIBLIOGRAPHY

Manuscript Sources
British Library
Add. MSS. 7966A
Add. MSS. 8835
Add. MSS. 17362
Add. MSS. 22923
Add. MSS. 25459
Add. MSS. 26891
Add. MSS. 35093
MS. Cotton Cleopatra D IX
MS. Cotton Faustina B V; VI
MS. Cotton Nero C VIII; D X
MS. Cotton Tiberius E VIII
MS. Harl. 46 A43
MS. Stowe 553

Public Record Office
E101 9/23
E101 15/2
E101 17/211-13
E101 360/10
E101 363/18
E101 368/8
E101 375/9-20
E101 379/4
E101 492/21
E101 531/17
E142 56
SC6 1145-8
SC6 1148/13
SC11 279

Printed Sources
Calendar of Chancery Warrants 1244-1326

Calendar of Charter Rolls 1300-1326
Calendar of Close Rolls 1302-1377
Calendar of Documents Relating to Scotland 1272-1357
Calendar of Fine Rolls 1272-1327
Calendar of Papal Letters 1305-1342
Calendar of Patent Rolls 1281-1330
Hist. MSS. Comm. 11th Report, App. pt. 3.
Rotuli Parliamentorum
Statutes of the Realm

Secondary Sources

Altschul, M., *A Baronial Family in Medieval England: The Clares, 1217-1314* (Baltimore, 1965).

Aungier, G. J., (ed.) *Chroniques de London* (Camden Soc. 28, 1844).

Babington, C. and Lumby, J. R., (eds.) *Polychronicon of Ranulph Higden* (9 vols., Rolls Series, London, 1865-86).

Barrow, G. S., *Robert Bruce* (London, 1965).

Barrow, G. S., 'Robert the Bruce 1329-1979', *History Today*, 29, 12 (1979) pp. 808-15.

Beardwood, A., *Records of the Trial of Walter Langeton, Bishop of Coventry and Lichfield 1307-1312* (Camden Soc. 4th series, 6, 1969).

Bingham, C., *The Life and Times of Edward II* (London, 1973).

Blackley, F.D., 'Adam, The Bastard Son of Edward II', *Bulletin of the Inst. HR.*, 37 (1964), pp. 76-7.

Blackley, F. D., and Hermansen G., (eds.) *The Household Book of Queen Isabella of England* (Alberta, 1971).

Blaauw, W. H., 'Letters of Edward, Prince of Wales', *Sussex Arch. Collections*, 2, (1849) pp. 80-98.

Bond, E. A., (ed.) *Chronica Monasterii de Melsa* (3 vols., Rolls Series, London, 1866-8).

Boswell, J., *Christianity, Social Tolerance and Homosexuality* (Chicago, 1980).

Bradbury, J., *The Medieval Archer* (Woodbridge, 1985).

Bradbury, J., *The Medieval Siege* (Woodbridge, 1992).

Broome, D., 'Exchequer Migrations to York in the Thirteenth and Fourteenth Centuries', Little, A. G. and Powicke, F. M., *Essays in Medieval History Presented to T. F. Tout*, pp. 291-300 (Manchester, 1925).

Brundage, J. A., *Law, Sex and Christian Society in Medieval Europe* (Chicago, 1987).

Buck, M., *Politics, Finance and the Church in the Reign of Edward II* (Cambridge, 1983).

Buck, M., 'The Reform of the Exchequer 1316-1326', *English Hist. Review*, 98 (1983) pp. 241-60.

Byerly, B. F. and Byerly, C. R., (eds.) *Records of the Wardrobe and Household 1285-6* (London, 1977).

Byerly, B. F. and Byerly, C. R., (eds.) *Records of the Wardrobe and Household 1286-9* (London, 1986).

Chaplais, P., *The War of Saint Sardos* (Camden Soc. 3rd series, 87, 1954).

Chaplais, P., (ed.) *Treaty Rolls* (London, 1955).

Chaplais, P., *Piers Gaveston, Edward II's Adoptive Brother* (Oxford, 1994).

Childs, W. R. and Taylor, J., *The Anominalle Chronicle 1307-1334* (Leeds, 1991).

Clanchy, M. T., *From Memory to Written Record* (2nd ed., Oxford, 1993).

Clarke, M., *Medieval Representation and Consent* (Oxford, 1936).

Colvin, H. M., *The History of the King's Works* (6 vols., London, 1953).

Contamine, P., *War in the Middle Ages* (Oxford, 1984).

Cooper, W. D., *The History of Winchelsea* (London, 1850).

Cuttino, G. P., and Lyman, T.W., 'Where is Edward II?', *Speculum*, 53 (1978) pp. 522-539.

Davies, J. C., 'The Despenser War in Glamorgan', *T.R.H.S.* 3rd series, 9 (1915) pp. 21-64.

Davies, J. C., *The Baronial Opposition to Edward II* (Cambridge, 1918).

Davies, R. R., *Lordship and Society in the March of Wales 1282-1400* (Oxford, 1978).

Denholm-Young, N., (ed.) *The Life of Edward the Second* (London, 1957).

Devon, F., *Issues of the Exchequer* (London, 1837).

Dickinson, W. C. and Duncan, A. A. M., *Scotland from the Earliest Times to 1603* (Oxford, 1977).

Dimock, J. F., *Opera Giraldi Cambrensis* (8 vols., Rolls Series, London, 1861-91).

Druon, M., *The Iron King* (London, 1956).

Du Boulay, F. R. H., *The Lordship of Canterbury* (London, 1966).

Duncan, A. A. M., (ed.) *The Acts of Robert I, King of Scots 1306-29* (Edinburgh, 1988).

Eckhardt, C. D., (ed.) *Castleford's Chronicle* (2 vols., Oxford, 1996).

Edwards, K., 'The Political Importance of the English Bishops During the Reign of Edward II', *English Hist. Review*, 59 (1944) pp. 311-347.

Forker, C. R., (ed.) *Edward the Second* (Manchester, 1994).

Frolich, W., *St Anselm* (3 vols., Kalamazoo, 1990-4).

Fryde, E. B., 'The Deposits of Hugh Despenser the Younger with Italian Bankers', *Econ. Hist. Rev.*, 2nd series, 3 (1951), pp. 344-62.

Fryde, N., *The Tyranny and Fall of Edward II 1321-1326* (Cambridge, 1979).

Gardner, A., *Documents Relating to Edward I* (London, 1888).

Graham, R.,(ed.) *The Register of Robert Winchelsey, Archbishop of Canterbury* (2 vols. Oxford, 1952-6).

Gransden, A., (ed.) *The Chronicle of Bury St Edmunds 1212-1301* (London, 1964).

Gransden, A., *Historical Writing in England* (2 vols., London, 1974, 1982).

Gransden, A., The Chronicles of Medieval England and Scotland, *Journal of Medieval History*, 16 (1990) pp. 129-50; 17 (1991) pp. 217-42).

Graves, R., *English and Scottish Ballads* (London, 1957).

Green, M. A. E., *Lives of the Princesses of England* (6 vols., London, 1849-51).

Hall, H., (ed.) *The Red Book of the Exchequer* (3 vols., Rolls Series, London, 1896).

Hamilton, J., *Piers Gaveston, Earl of Cornwall, 1307-12* (Detroit, 1988).

Hardy, T. D., (ed.) *Rymer's Foedera* (3 vols., London, 1869-85)

Hart, W. H., (ed.) *Historia et Cartularium Monasterii Sancti Petri Gloucestrie* (3 vols., Rolls Series, London, 1863-7).

Haskins, G. L., 'A Chronicle of the Civil Wars of Edward II', *Speculum*, 14 (1939) pp. 73-8.

Heath, P., *Church and Realm 1272-1461* (London, 1988).

Hector, L. C. and Harvey, B., (eds.) *The Westminster Chronicle 1381-1394* (Oxford, 1982).

Hingeston-Randolph, F. C., (ed.) *The Register of Walter de Stapledon, Bishop of Exeter 1307-1326* (London and Exeter, 1892).

Holinshed, R., *Chronicles of England* (6 vols, London, 1807).

Hutchison, H., 'Edward II and his Minions', *History Today*, 21, 8 (1971) pp. 542-9.

Johnstone, H., (ed.) *Letters of Edward, Prince of Wales* (Edinburgh, 1931).

Johnstone, H., 'The Eccentricities of Edward II', *English Hist. Review*, 48 (1933) pp. 264-7.

Johnstone, H., 'Isabella, the She-Wolf of France', *History*, 21 (1936) pp. 208-18).

Johnstone, H., *Edward of Caernarvon* (Manchester, 1946).

Keen, M. H., *England in the Later Middle Ages* (London, 1973).

Knight, J., 'Newport Castle', *Monmouthshire Antiquary*, 7, (1991).

Latham, R. E., (ed.) *Memoranda Rolls 1326-7* (London, 1968).

Leader, D. H., *A History of the University of Cambridge* (Cambridge, 1988).

Levison, W, (ed.) 'St Edmundsbury Chronicle', *English Hist. Review*, 58 (1943) pp. 51-78).

Luard, H, R., (ed.) *Annales Monastici* (5 vols., Rolls Series, London, 1857-69).

Luard, H.R., (ed.) *Flores Historiarum* (3 vols., Rolls Series, London, 1890).

Lucas, H. S., 'The Great European Famine of 1315, 1316 and 1317', *Speculum*, 5 (1930) pp. 343-77.

Lumby, J.R., (ed.) *The Chronicles of Henry Knighton* (2 vols., Rolls Series, London, 1889).

Macaulay, G. C., (ed.) *The Chronicles of Froissart*, (London, 1924).

Maddicott, J.R., *Thomas of Lancaster 1307-1322* (Oxford, 1970).

Madox, T., (ed.) *The History and Antiquities of the Exchequer* (2 vols., London, 1749).

Maxwell, H., (ed.) *The Chronicle of Lanercost 1272-1346* (Glasgow, 1913).

McKisack, M., *The Fourteenth Century* (Oxford, 1959).

Murray Smith, A,. *The Roll-Call of Westminster Abbey* (London, 1912).

Ormrod, W., 'Edward II at Neath Abbey, 1326', *Neath Antiquarian Society Transactions* (1988-9) pp. 107-112.

Page, W., (ed.) *Victoria County History of Derbyshire* (2 vols., London, 1905-7).

Page, W., (ed.) *Victoria County History of Hertfordshire* (4 vols., London, 1908).

Page, W., (ed.) *Victoria County History of Cornwall* (2 vols., 1906-24).

Palgrave, F., (ed.) *Kalendars and Inventories of the Exchequer* (3 vols., London, 1836).

Parsons, D., (ed.) *Eleanor of Castile 1290-1990* (Stamford, 1991).

Pearce, E, H., (ed.) *The Register of Thomas de Cobham Bishop of Worcester 1317-27* (Worcester Historical Society, 1930).

Phillips, J., *Aymer de Valence* (Oxford, 1972).

Poole, R, L., *Chronicles and Annals* (Oxford, 1926).

Prestwich, M., *Three Edwards: War and State in England, 1272-1377* (London, 1980).

Prestwich, M., *Edward I* (London, 1988).

Raine, J., (ed.) *Papers and Letters from the Northern Registers* (Rolls Series, London, 1873).

Renouard, Y., (ed.) *Gascon Rolls 1307-17*, (London, 1962).

Riley, H. T., (ed.) *Liber Custumarum in Munimenta Guildhallae Londiniensis* (2 vols., Rolls Series, London, 1860).

Riley, H. T., (ed.) *The Chronicle of Thomas Walsingham* (2 vols., Rolls Series, London, 1863-4).

Riley, H. T., (ed.) W. Rishanger, *Chronica et Annales* (Rolls Series, London, 1865).

Riley, H. T., (ed.) *Johannis de Trokelowe et Henrici de Blaneforde Chronici et Annales* (Rolls Series, 1866).

Roberts, R. A., 'Edward II, the Lords Ordainers and Piers Gaveston's Jewels and Horses (1312-1313)', *Camden Misc.*, 15, (1929) pp. 1-26.

Rothwell, H., (ed.) *The Chronicle of Walter of Guisborough* (Camden 3rd series, 89, 1955-6).

Royal Commission of Historic Monuments (England) *An Inventory of the Historical Monuments in Hertfordshire* (London, 1911).

Sandys, A., 'The Financial and Administrative Importance of the London Temple in the Thirteenth Century', Little, A. G. and Powicke, F. M.,

Essays in Medieval History Presented to T. F. Tout, pp. 147-62 (Manchester, 1925).

Rutherford, E,. *Sarum,* (London, 1987).

Sayles, G. O., 'The Formal Judgements on the Traitors of 1322', *Speculum,* 16 (1941) pp. 57-63.

Sheppard, J. B., (ed.) *Canterbury Letters* (3 vols., Rolls Series, London, 1898).

Skeat, W., *The Bruce* (Early English Text Society, 2 vols., London, 1870, 1889).

Southern, R. W., *Saint Anselm and his Biographer* (Cambridge, 1966).

Stapleton, T. S., 'A Brief Summary of the Wardrobe Accounts of the 10th, 11th and 14th years of Edward II', *Archaeologia,* 26 (1836) pp. 318-345.

Stevenson, J., (ed.) *Chronicon de Lanercost* (Edinburgh,1839).

Stones, E. L. G., 'The Date of Roger Mortimer's Escape from the Tower' in *English. Hist. Review,* 66 (1951) pp. 97-8.

Stones, E. L. G., *Anglo-Scottish Relations 1174-1328* (London, 1965).

Stow, J., *The Chronicles of England from Brute unto this Present Yeare,* (London, 1580).

Strickland, A., *Lives of the Queens of England* (8 vols., London, 1885).

Stubbs, W., (ed.) *Chronicles of the Reigns of Edward I and Edward II* (2 vols., Rolls Series, London, 1882-3).

Tanquerey, F. J., 'The Conspiracy of Thomas Dunheved, 1327', *English Hist. Review,* 31 (1916) pp. 119-124.

Taylor, A. J., 'Building at Caerphilly in 1326', *Bulletin of the Board of Celtic Studies,* 14 (1952) pp. 299-300.

Taylor, J., *The Universal Chronicle of Ranulf Higden* (Oxford, 1966).

Thompson, E. M., (ed.) *The Chronicle of Adam Murimuth* (Rolls Series, London, 1889).

Topham, J., (ed.) *Liber Quotidianus Contrarotularis Garderobae* (London, 1787).

Tout, T. F., *The English Civil Service in the Fourteenth Century* (Manchester, 1916).

Tout, T. F., *Collected Papers* (3 vols., Manchester, 1934).

Tout, T. F., *The Place of Edward II in English History* (Manchester, 1914, 1936).

Tout, T. F., *Chapters in Medieval Administrative History* (6 vols., Manchester, 1923-35).

Tuck, A., *Crown and Nobility* (London, 1985).

Tupling, G. H., *South Lancashire in the Reign of Edward II,* (Chetham Soc. 3rd series, 1, 1949).

Upton-Ward, J. M., (ed.) *The Templars* (Woodbridge, 1992).

Waugh, S., *The Lordship of England, Royal Wardships and Marriage in English Society and Politics 1217-1327* (Princeton, 1988).

Wright, T., *Political Songs of England* (Camden Soc. 6, 1839). (Reprinted: Coss, P. (ed.) *Thomas Wright's Political Songs of England* (Cambridge, 1996).

Wright, T., (ed.) *The Roll of Caerlaverock* (London, 1864).

Wright, T., (ed.) *The Chronicle of Pierre de Langtoft* (2 vols., Rolls Series, London, 1866).

INDEX

Buchard, Thomas, 60, 80

Building and architecture, 8-9, 32-3, 38-9, 42, 71, 112-3

Burgh-by-sands (Cumb.), death of Edward I at, 29

Burghersh, Henry, Bishop of Lincoln, 119-121

Burton-upon-Trent (Staffs), 109

Bury St Edmunds (Suff.), abbey, 16-17

Byfleet (Surrey), 32-3, 113

Caerlaverock (Scotland), castle, 18, song of, 17-18

Caernarvon, 5, castle, 6, 103, 115

Caerphilly (Glam.), castle, 83, 104, 133-4

Cambridge, King's Hall, 91

Cambridgeshire, 81

Canterbury (Kent), mint at, 48, Isabella at, 107, 123

Cardiff, 83, 102, 104

Carisbrooke (Isle of Wight), castle, 47

Carlisle (Cumb.), 16-7, 23, 28-9, 37, 80, 115

Carlisle, Andrew Harclay, Earl of, 110, 117

Carrickfergus (Ireland), 80

Castle Rising (Norf.), 144-5

Chamber, King's, 3, 113

Chancery, 3, 60-1

Chaplais, Pierre, 2

Charles IV, King of France, 117, 121, 127

Charles de Valois, brother of Philip IV, 44

Chepstow (Mon.), castle, 132

Chester, castle, 20-1, earldom of, 20, 69

Cinque ports, 18, 66, 107

Cirencester (Glos.), 109

Clare, Eleanor of, Lady Despenser, 28, 60, 77, 116. 131

Clare, Elizabeth of, m. a) Theobald Verdon, b) John Burgh, c) Roger Damory, 77

Clare, Gilbert of, Earl of Gloucester, m. Joan of Acre, 7

Clare, Gilbert of, Earl of Gloucester, 22, 67, regent, 52, 70, death at Bannockburn, 76, inheritance, 77, 88

Clare, Margaret of, m. a) Piers Gavaston, 38, 61, b) Hugh Audley, 77

Clement V, Pope, 48, 70, 86, dissolution of the Templars, 57

Cobham, Thomas, Bishop of Worcester, 71, 100

Comyn, John, 16, 26, 28

Comyn, William, 7

Contrariants, 113-4, 119, 120

Conwy (Caern.), castle, 19, 126

Corfe (Dorset.), castle, 138, 143-4

Cornwall, earldom of, 30, 38, 46

Crab, John, engineer, 95-6

Cromwell, John, keeper of the Tower of London, 68, 88

Croydon (Surrey), 42, 132

Crossbowmen, 24, 95, 116

Damory, Roger, 77, 87-8, 99, 104, 108, 110

Dampierre, Guy of, Count of Flanders, 13-14

Dean, Forest of (Glos.), 75, 83

Deddington (Oxon), 63-64

Despenser, Hugh, the elder, 87, 100, 103, Earl of Winchester, 112, banished, 106-7, recalled, 109, death, 133

Despenser, Hugh, the younger, 33, 81, 83, 87-100, m. Eleanor of

Clare, 28, estates in Wales, 102-3, rebellion against, 104, banished, 106-7, recalled, 109, Chamberlain, 113, death, 134

Dominicans, 27-8, 50, 53, 64-5

Dordrecht (Holland), 130

Dover (Kent), Edward II at, 34, 39, 69, 123-4, castle, 65, 126, 129

Dumfries (Scotland), 18, 37

Dunbar (Scotland), 15, 76

Dundalk (Ireland), 80

Dunhead, Thomas, 138

Dunstable (Beds.), priory, 9-10

Edinburgh, 75

Edward the Confessor: King of England, 6, regalia of, 43

Edward I, King of England: and Gavaston, 34, in Scotland, 15-19, 23-6, death, 29

Edward II, King of England: birth, 5, character, 1-3, 100, marriage plans, 12-14, Prince of Wales, 20-9, coronation, 42-5, marriage, 39, and the Templars, 58-9, in France, 39, 69, 99, in Scotland, 17, 51-2, 74-6, 115-116, flight, 130, imprisonment, 136-140, death, 140-1, proposed canonization, 142

Edward III, King of England: birth, 69, betrothal, 130, coronation, 143

Eleanor, daughter of Edward I, 5, 7

Eleanor of Acquitaine, Queen of Henry II, 13

Eleanor of Castile, Queen of Edward I, 5, 9, 10

Eleanor of Provence, Queen of Henry III, 7, 11

Eleanor of Woodstock, daughter of Edward II, 94, 145

Elizabeth, daughter of Edward I, 5, 27

Eltham (Kent), 69, 86

Ely (Cambs.), cathedral, 72

Eric, King of Norway, 12

Exchequer, 3, 51, 55, 61, 91, 114

Famine of 1315-17, 79

Ferrer, Guy, tutor, 8

Fieschi, Luke, Cardinal, 87, 92

Fille, Richard, keeper of the River Thames, 131

French Chronicle of London, 131

Frescobaldi, Amerigo dei, 22, 48, 55

Froissart, Jean, chronicle of, 123, 129, 134

Frowick, Roger, goldsmith, 43

Galloway (Scotland), 18

Gascony, 13, 39, 48, 70, 117-8, 124

Gaucelin of Eauze, Cardinal, 87, 92

Gavaston, Piers, Earl of Cornwall: early career, 22-3, 29-36, marriage, 38, regent, 39-40, coronation of Edward II, 43-4, attacked by the Ordainers, 46. 54, exiled, 47, 62, recalled, 49, 60, capture, 63, death and funeral, 64-5

Gerald of Wales, 21

Glamorgan, 102-4, 133

Glastonbury (Som.) abbot of, 103

Gloucester, 104, 109, 132-3, 138, St. Peter's Abbey, 141-2

Gloucester, Earls of, *see* Clare.

Gloucestershire, 92, 104, 114

Gower, 102-3, 134

Grampian mountains, 52

Guardians of Scotland, 12-16

Guildford (Surrey), 32, 124, 144